Me
BEFORE
ANYONE ELSE

SELF-IMPROVEMENT

FRANK TAYLOR

Me Before Everyone Else Mindset

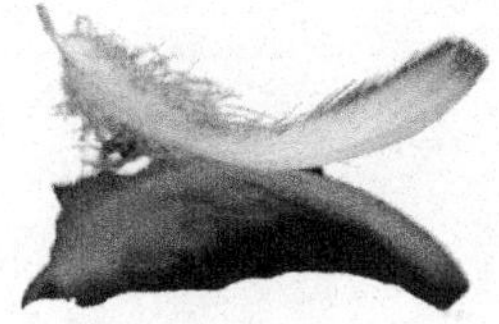

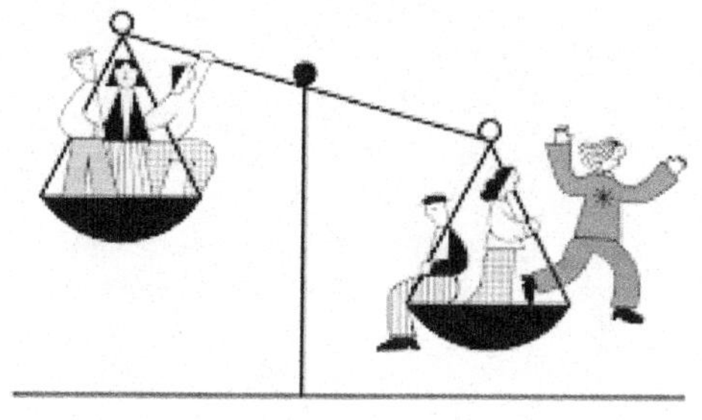

By

Francis L.

About the Author

Francis is a passionate writer and adept company director currently managing 5000 employees. He holds a degree in Business Administration. And his unique quality to explore human psychology and how they react in different scenarios has prompted him to write this book. His keen observation and unbiased analysis of society are unparalleled, and the information conveyed in the book is precise and unique. Most people were taken aback in the wake of the pandemic, but not Francis. He made the utmost of the opportunity and came up with ways to cope with this pandemic in the best ways possible. Self-esteem and self-worth are traits of the personality he considers of utmost significance. He delves deeper into the topic with pragmatic approaches so that you can understand the subject matter without breaking a sweat.

TABLE OF CONTENT

Introduction

The world is battling with an intangible, lethal adversary, attempting to comprehend how to live with the danger presented by a virus, which is invisible to the naked eye. According to some authors, the only way ahead is to put pen to paper and attempt to comprehend and describe what it feels like to continue living in a world when nations are under lockdown, and normal life seems to have come to a grinding stop.

As the coronavirus epidemic has spread over the globe, it has prompted a slew of journal entries and essays describing how life has altered as a result. Novelists, critics, artists, and journalists have all attempted to put into words the emotions that many people are experiencing. As a consequence, we have a first draught of how we will remember this period in the future, which is filled with uncertainty, anguish, and dread, as well as brief glimpses of hope and humanity.

A feeling of disarray pervades the serene calm, as if society has been thrown out of whack and that the old norms no longer apply. Small groups of pedestrians stand in the shadows as though they are part of an audience watching a show that is slowly emerging. People take a moment to rest on street corners and in the shade of trees, all under the careful eye of paramilitary troops and law enforcement officers.

There are some individuals who have imaginations that are inspired only by what they can see; I blame this narrow-minded empiricism for the parks that are overflowing with people and the pubs that were packed up until a few nights ago. My imagination, on the other hand, is very different. I am terrified of anything that is not apparent to me. Observing the suffering from the safety of my home, I am terrified of what I cannot see: people running out of money and food, individuals drowning in fluid in their lungs, and the deaths of healthcare staff who are now becoming sick while doing their responsibilities. I am concerned about the federal government, which the right-wing has deliberately debilitated to the point that it is not only unable to assist its citizens but is actively obstructing assistance from reaching them.I'm worried that we won't be able to punish the right enough. I'm afraid of leaving home and maybe spreading the illness. I'm concerned about what this period of terror is doing to my children, their imaginations, and their souls, among other things.

As a result of the shutdown, the activities that define our days—commuting to work, bringing our children to school, having a drink with friends—disappear, and time seems to have a flat, smooth appearance. It's easy to feel a bit disjointed when you don't have some kind of framework in place.

Giving time a structure is particularly vital at this moment when the future seems to be so ill-defined. We have no way of knowing if the infection will continue to rampage for weeks, months, or, lord, helps us, for years on end.We don't know for sure. It's impossible to predict when we'll be able to relax.And so many of us, with the exception of those who are adept at compartmentalization or denial, continues to be essentially captives of our own anxieties. Our lives, our lengthy days spent with ourselves, our spouses, or our family, may continue in this state if we do not generate at least the idea of movement in our lives.

How the Coronavirus and the ensuing lockdown have resulted in people's low self-esteem, low self-respect, and low confidence will be discussed in length in this book. As someone who has dealt with all of these issues firsthand, I can sympathise with those who are. This book will present you with a wealth of knowledge on how to maintain your humility, productivity, and composure in these dire times.

Chapter 1

Self-Respect And Self Esteem Is Affected During COVID-19

The COVID-19 pandemic epidemic is widely regarded as the worst pandemic outbreak in modern history. The COVID-19 epidemic has had a substantial influence on the general public's psychological well-being. As a result, the monitoring and oversight of the mental health of the community during emergencies such as a pandemic is a top concern right away. These findings, as well as the implications for future investigations, will be used to examine and evaluate previous research on how the COVID-19 epidemic affected people's stress, anxiety and depression. COVID-19 not only causes physical health problems but it also has the potential to induce a variety of psychiatric issues. The transmission of the novel coronavirus has the potential to have an influence on the mental health of people in many areas. As a result, it is critical to maintaining individual mental health while also developing psychological therapies that can improve the mental health of susceptible populations throughout the COVID-19 pandemic.

When faced with adversity, our self-esteem determines how we respond. It is not how others treat us, but how we treat ourselves and the rest of the world that matters.

Until now, we've never had to cope with a world as unpleasant as this one. Because of this, it should come as no surprise that experiencing such a great deal of turmoil may have a negative effect on our self-esteem. Many people have lost their jobs or are facing an uncertain future as a result of the epidemic and lockdown, which has also resulted in problematic family relationships, which has resulted in damaged egos and poor self-esteem. Many people find it difficult to summon the self-motivation to pick up the pieces of their lives and start over. It has evolved into a concern for the majority of people's well-being.

It is this battle with a new way of living that has resulted in a growing sense of loneliness in my life. The fact that some people turn to social media in search of affirmation or reassurance might have the opposite impact on their self-esteem. Using social media can be comforting, especially if you use it to keep in touch with long-distance friends and relatives or to stay in touch with a large social circle while the school is closed. I don't want to imply that social media is always a bad thing; on the contrary, it can be a source of comfort. However, even during these trying times, being on social media has the ability to influence the thoughts of millions of people.

Emotional turmoil is only barely discernible. The effort and sorrow of a person who is suffering within are invisible to others around them. When someone is depressed, they may begin to think that they are useless and undeserving of anything.

No judgment we make on ourselves is more essential than the one we cast on others: how we see ourselves affects the basic foundation of our existence. Self-esteem is believed to be the most important factor in living a meaningful life; it simply relates to how we perceive ourselves – whether positively or negatively. Self-esteem is not a luxury, but rather a psychological quality that must be nurtured and developed. If you have a healthy sense of self-worth, your thoughts about yourself will frequently be positive, you will feel good about yourself, and you will believe that you are deserving of other people's respect. You may go through tough periods in your life, but you will normally be able to deal with them in a positive manner and without them having a significant negative influence on your long-term well-being.

With low self-esteem, your perceptions about yourself are generally negative, and you place little importance on your own opinions and ideas, which can lead to depression. You will have a tendency to concentrate on your flaws or shortcomings, and you may find it difficult to acknowledge the great aspects of your personality. You may also hold yourself responsible for any troubles or failures that you have had in the past.

Self-esteem is a specific manner of feeling one's own personhood or identity. And if that ego is at war with itself as a result of external pressure, then existence is filled with sorrow. As we grow up, we expect to be well-adjusted individuals who can achieve their objectives and deal with challenges with relative ease. This is based on our level of education and parental supervision. However, this isn't always the situation. When we experience particular hurdles in our lives, we often come to understand a great deal about our own personal shortcomings and inner strengths. When faced with adversity, our self-esteem determines how we respond. It is not how others treat us that matters, but how we treat ourselves and the rest of the world.

The World Health Organization (WHO) declared the coronavirus pandemic on March 11, 2020, the first day of the year 2020, which was the first day of the year 2020..

Following an increase in the reported incidence of COVID-19 cases, many nations implemented partial and comprehensive lockdowns, with stringent shutdowns believed to have saved about 3 million lives. Along with measures such as quarantine of sick individuals, the use of masks, and maintaining social distance, most schools and colleges were closed, and online teaching methods were used to provide instruction. COVID-19 has caused critical mental health services throughout the world to be disrupted at a time when they are most needed. During and after the epidemic, world leaders must act swiftly and decisively to increase investment in life-saving mental health programs in order to save more lives. The pandemic has far-reaching consequences for large populations and health-care systems alike. A worldwide economic crisis has been sparked by the interruption of trade routes and the imposition of restrictions to the free movement of people and products at the same time.

It is vitally essential to one's total health and well-being to maintain good mental health. Around the world, the COVID-19 epidemic kept over 300 million school pupils, as well as many other people, at home. Even if there are differing views on the usefulness of keeping children at home, school closing choices are believed to be the safest option across the world. Consequently, pupils' educational journeys have been unpredictable and significantly disrupted as a result of the virus' containment.

There has been a number of researches conducted on the long- and short-term consequences of the pandemic on the social and psychological well-being of the community. People's behaviour and mental health have been determined to have been significantly impacted by the COVID-19 pandemic, according to a huge number of studies. According to some study, this is not the case at all.. The number of calls to mental health hotlines in the United States increased by 1,000 per cent during the period when more people were placed under lockdown as a result of the epidemic.

Nervousness and anxiety are widespread in today's culture and impact almost everyone to some degree. A growing body of research demonstrates that people who are placed in isolation and quarantine feel elevated levels of anxiety as well as rage and disorientation . The majority of the studies that have looked into psychological disorders related to the COVID-19 pandemic have found that the affected individuals exhibit a variety of symptoms of mental trauma, including emotional distress and depression, stress and mood swings, irritability and insomnia, attention deficit hyperactivity disorder, post-traumatic stress disorder, and anger. It has also been discovered via research that frequent media exposure might create discomfort. Nonetheless, in the current environment, it is difficult to forecast with accuracy the psychological and emotional implications of COVID-19. A recent study carried out in China, which was the first country to be afflicted by the current Virus outbreak, revealed that people's anxiety over being exposed to an unknown virus might result in mental illnesses.

It is possible that COVID-19 will have an effect on the mental health of a wide range of people in society, including those who are infected and those who work in health care as well as those in families, schools, and other settings, as well as those who suffer from mental illness.

It was felt necessary to undertake a systematic assessment of the available research in this area in order to present a holistic but complete statistics on how COVID-19 affects general population mental health, as well as a worldwide shortage in data on the issue. To explore and carefully review and analyze the literature and their stated results linked to the effects of COVID-19 on the prevalence of stress, anxiety, and depression, this study has been designed to do so. Due to the uncertainty surrounding these outcomes, COVID-19 has a significant negative impact on students' academic progress, social life at college, and future professions, among other things. Not only were people at danger of illness and death, but they were also under a lot of stress due to the pandemic's psychological toll. Even prior to the outbreak, students all around the world were experiencing increased levels of worry, melancholy moods, psychosomatic difficulties, and a lack of self-esteem. As a result of heightened worry, stress, and sadness, students may require additional resources and assistance to handle the physical and mental health consequences of their experiences.

Some of the previously recognised psychological effects of COVID-19 on students were re-examined in a more recent study. Due to changes in teaching methods and a lack of clarity about the value of university education, many students are experiencing greater levels of stress, depression, and anxiety. These concerns, combined with technological concerns about virtual teaching, being away from home, decreased family income and social isolation, as well as future employment, have been observed in universities around the world.

The effects of pandemics on people's mental health such as psychological discomfort, anxiety, depression, and low self-esteem, differ from one nation to the next. For example, according to a study performed in Italy, 15.4 percent of the population suffers from a very high degree of melancholy, 11.5 percent suffers from severe levels of anxiety, and 12.6 percent suffer from significant stress.

According to the definition, self-esteem is defined as the connection between an individual's ideal and real self-concept. A person's sense of self-worth is associated with a variety of psychological outcomes, including psychological adjustment and prosocial conduct, and may be categorized into two categories: high and low self-esteem. High self-esteem is defined by a strong sense of confidence and belief in one's own abilities, as well as a high level of pleasure with one's own appearance. Low self-esteem is defined by a lack of self-assurance as well as a tendency to feel awful about one's own appearance. 11 Research has confirmed that poor self-esteem is connected with harmful habits and practices. 12 When compared to persons who have high self-esteem, people who have low self-esteem are more likely to suffer from mental health difficulties.

OVID-19 is a very stressful and distressing event, and stressful situations may have a significant impact on one's mental health and well-being. According to a statement on the International OCD Foundation website, researchers from the Genomic Psychiatry Cohort studied patients with OCD and BDD to determine whether there were any changes in rates of traumatic event exposure across the groups. Individuals suffering from both BDD and OCD reported a significantly greater rate of exposure to at least one stressful incident, according to the study.

During the year that COVID-19 has disrupted the notion of normalcy and raged around the world, individuals have had more opportunity to reflect on their own self-worth.

Contrary to popular belief and belief, several researchers have shown that self-esteem has little or no influence on illness preventive and treatment behavior. Despite the fact that research on the relationship between self-esteem and health status and health preventative practices have come up with no convincing results, they do show a favorable relationship. As a result, the correlations between the perceived danger of COVID-19, the perceived efficacy of the reaction to the threat, and the fear elicited by the disease were explored in this study. Additionally, the moderating effects of self-esteem traits (such as having a high vs a low self-esteem) on these correlations were looked into.

Health habits in groups with certain demographic features, such as age and gender, have been explored and compared in previous research. According to the findings of this study, age is defined as the length of time a person has spent on this planet. The health habits of teenagers and young adults have been found to differ significantly in several research studies. Distinct age groups have different impacts on the sense-making process as a consequence of age stereotypes, which leads in variances in self-perceived health behaviors as a result of age stereotypes. Particularly when it comes to gender, it refers to the physical condition of being either male or female in nature. For example, in young people in the United States, the authors found that 40 percent of males engaged in harmful behavior (e.g., bad nutrition), compared to just 22 percent of girls. Some researchers, on the other hand, have found no indication of a relationship between gender and the practice of harmful activities. The association between gender and health behavior found in earlier research prompted the inclusion of both age and gender in this study's analysis of COVID-19 preventive activities among the participants. Depression is a critical condition that affects the quality of a person's life by creating emotional, physical, and behavioral changes.Any stage of a person's life, from birth to old age, can be affected by anxiety symptoms. It was designed in 1965 as a 20-item self-report assessment tool to measure depression levels. The ZSDS is a self-report assessment tool that measures depression levels. Normal, mild, moderate, and severe depression are the four stages of depression measured by the total depression index score, which runs from 25 to 100.

Self-Esteem is one of the depression-related aspects that must be addressed in order to be effective in psychiatric treatments. Over the course of the last century, health researchers have looked at the relationship between self-esteem and depression in great detail.

As defined by the American Psychological Association, self-esteem is a specific attitude and perspective of oneself that influences interactions and sentiments toward oneself and others. In therapeutic and research practise, the Rosenberg Self-Esteem Scale (RSES) is an important 10-item standardised resource. It was developed by Dr. Rosenberg himself. The overall amount of the scoring varies between 10 and 40 points. The mean of the total score is used as the key indication in the majority of research that employ RSES. In the RSES, the findings are presented in two categories: low and high. The majority of research paid little attention to the subjects' self-esteem levels, and only a few studies used the subjects' self-esteem levels to compare groups of participants in order to determine internal consistency. According to research, depression is exacerbated when one's self-esteem is low. In addition, a great deal of study has been done on the interaction between depression and self-esteem in order to determine whether or not there is a causal relationship between depression and self-esteem.

According to recent research, low self-esteem is a negative predictor of depression.

It's rare for university students to have research done on the link between depression and low self-esteem. Our understanding does not include any studies that have examined the association between depression and self-esteem among university students during the COVD-19 epidemic, which would be of interest to us. In order to assess students' psychological well-being, educational institutions must conduct assessments of their own.

During the COVID-19 epidemic, this research investigated the relationship between pupils' self-esteem and depression. Also investigated is the association between poor self-esteem and depression, as well as whether low levels of self-esteem are connected with depressive symptoms among university students who are participating in the study.

The cut-off points were used to assess the levels of self-esteem and depression in the participants. The degree of self-esteem among male and female students is depicted in the following table. Eighty-nine percent (59 percent) of the respondents have strong self-esteem, whereas 62 percent (41 percent) have poor self-esteem. A statistically significant greater proportion of high-level self-esteem is found in both male and female students, although female students have a statistically significant larger percentage of high-level self-esteem than male students.This is true regardless of whether or not the student is male or female.Table 2 shows a summary of the results based on the gender of the students who participated in the same depression level analysis as in Table 1. "Mild depression," "Moderate depression," and "Severe depression" were experienced by 57 (30.7 percent), 31 (20.5 percent), and 25 (16.6 percent) of those who answered the survey questions. According to the data in the table, 29 percent of female students suffered from severe depression, which is much higher than the 4 percent of male students who suffered from severe depression.

Chapter 2

Explaining Psychology of Self Respect And Self Esteem

Our concept of self is influenced in part by how we see ourselves. However, our perception of ourselves is also influenced by how we feel about ourselves, or, more simply put, how we regard ourselves.

That's the message we're continually bombarded with novels, television programmes, superhero comics, and other familiar myths and legends, as well.

The belief is instilled in us that we can do anything if we have trust in ourselves.

As we all know, we cannot achieve anything in the world merely by believing; if that were the case, a lot more youngsters would be flying in the sky above their garage roofs rather than being forced to wear casts for a few weeks!

However, we know that having a healthy sense of self-worth and a willingness to accept oneself for who you are is critical to achieving your goals in life, having fulfilling relationships, and being content. An optimistic view on life helps us believe in our skills and motivates us to follow out our plans, leading to satisfaction.

Studies have shown that our general well-being is closely linked to our sense of worth, and it is pivotal to keep this in mind while interacting with others, especially youngsters, who are still establishing their sense of self-worth.

What Is Self-Esteem and What Isn't It?

Even if you already know the answer, let's start at the beginning: what exactly is self-esteem?

A person's total perception of their own value and worth is referred to as their "self-esteem." How much a person values, admires, appreciates, or admires himself or herself may be gauged by this number.

Self-esteem is just one's attitude toward oneself. A "favourable or unfavourable attitude toward oneself" is how he put it.

Self-esteem is thought to be influenced by a number of variables, including:

- Genetics
- Personality
- Life is a series of encounters.

- Health, Age, and Thoughts are all factors to consider.
- In light of the surrounding social situation, it follows that other people's responses
- Adopting an attitude of self-criticism

Note that self-esteem is not a stable state of affairs. We can evaluate and enhance it since it is reshapable and quantifiable.

Psychology and Self-Esteem

There is little doubt that self-esteem is a trendy topic in psychology.Even Freud, who many believe to be the founder of psychology, had ideas at the core of his work when it came to self-esteem.

Psychologists have been trying to figure out what self-esteem is, how it grows (or doesn't), and what effects it has for a long time, and there's no hint that we'll ever figure it out!

In spite of the fact that we still have a long way to go in understanding self-esteem, we've been able to narrow down what it is and how it varies from other related constructs in the field. What distinguishes self-esteem from other self-directed qualities and moods is explained below.

Self-Concept and Self-Esteem

Even if one's self-esteem may be a part of one's self-concept, it is not the same. When we ponder the question, "Who am I?" we discover who we are." our self-concept is the answer we come up with. Being aware of one's own ideas, feelings, preferences, and behaviours is the capacity to identify the areas in which one excels and where one falls short.

In a nutshell, our notion of ourselves is our knowledge of who we are.

When it comes to self-esteem and image, there is a big difference.

Although it has a distinct connotation, self-image is another related phrase. It refers to how you see yourself. It may, however, be founded on incorrect and faulty perceptions about ourselves rather than fact. Whether or whether our self-image is in sync with objective reality or how we are seen by others, it is usually not.

Self-Esteem and Self-Worth

Self-esteem refers to our thoughts, feelings, and beliefs about ourselves, whereas self-worth is a universal understanding of our worth as human beings who deserve to be loved and cared for.

Self-confidence and self-esteem are two distinct concepts. People's trust in themselves and their capacity to handle obstacles is measured by their self-confidence.A self-esteem boost is more likely to come from outward achievement and value than from internal evaluations of self-worth, as you may have seen from this description.

Even if one has a high level of self-assurance in a specific area or subject, it is possible to lack a healthy sense of one's own worth or worthiness in general.

Self-Belief vs Self-Efficacy

Self-efficacy and self-esteem go hand in hand, but self-efficacy is not a substitute for self-esteem. It is a conviction in one's capacity to succeed at specific undertakings that are referred to as self-efficacy. My self-efficacy in basketball is excellent, while my self-efficacy in math is poor.

Instead than focusing on a broad feeling of value, self-efficacy has a more narrow emphasis.

Comparison between self-esteem and self-awareness

Last but not least, self-worth is not the same as self-compassion. In self-compassion, the focus is not on how we see ourselves but on how we treat ourselves. Kindness and forgiveness toward oneself are essential components of practicing self-compassion. Self-compassion may help us develop a positive self-perception, but it is not a substitute for positive self-perception in and of itself.

Examples of People with a High Sense of Self-Esteem

A person's level of self-esteem may be determined by a number of factors.

Being open to criticism, admitting errors, and being comfortable with both giving and accepting praises are all examples of these qualities.In another example, the speaker, performer, sound and movement are all in harmony.

It's not uncommon for people with a strong sense of self-worth to be outspoken, curious, and open about their life's journey. They may also take pleasure in the lighter side of life and are confident in their ability to exert themselves in social or personal situations.

Even if low self-esteem has gotten greater attention, the positive psychology movement has pushed high self-esteem to the fore. We now understand what it means to have a positive feeling of self and how to achieve it.

- Appreciate yourself and others; we've learned through research.
- Enjoy the process of personal growth and development, as well as the discovery of purpose and meaning in one's life.
- Possess the ability to go within and conceive of new ideas.
- Take responsibility for their own actions and only agree to follow the instructions of others when they agree with them.
- Allow yourself to accept others as they are while encouraging them to grow in self-esteem and a positive outlook.
- Are able to focus on resolving personal issues with ease.
- Have relationships that are based on mutual love and respect.
- Consistently strive to achieve your ideas in whatever you do in life.
- Speak out and let people know what they think and what they need, all while being calm and compassionate.
- Put out an effort to make a good difference in the lives of others.

Having a strong sense of self-worth may be determined in a number of ways. If, for example, you act assertively without any sense of guilt and are comfortable conversing with people, then you probably have a strong sense of self-worth.

- Instead of dwelling on the past, try to concentrate on the present.
- Don't think that you're better or worse than anybody else.
- Refuse to be manipulated by others.
- Maintain healthy relationships by acknowledging and embracing a broad spectrum of emotions, both good and negative.
- A healthy work-life balance includes time for recreation and relaxation.
- Take on new challenges and take calculated risks if you want to advance in your career.
- Take criticism in stride, remembering that you are developing and improving as a person regardless of what people think of you.
- Never be ashamed of who yourself, and don't be afraid to speak out about your loves and dislikes.

- Don't try to change or better other people; instead, accept them as they are.

Some excellent instances of strong self-esteem may be drawn from these attributes.

Assume that a very talented and hard-working student receives an unsatisfactory mark on a challenging test. Strong self-esteem means that she is more likely to blame her failure on circumstances such as not studying hard enough, a particularly tough set of questions, or just having a "bad" day. However, she doesn't conclude that being stupid will guarantee her failure on any future tests.

To avoid sinking into despair or giving up, someone with a strong sense of self-worth is more likely to face the facts, reflect critically on her failures, and devise new strategies for success.

Consider a young guy on his first date as a second example. Because he loves the girl, he's going out with, he wants to impress and connect with her in the best possible way. While on the date, he discovers that she is driven by very distinct ideals, with quite different preferences in practically every aspect of her life.

He's not scared to share his own thoughts and ideas rather than just agreeing with what she has to say. Because of his great self-esteem, he is able to maintain open communication with others, even when they do not share his ideals. It's more essential to him to be himself than to try to win over his date.

What are the difficulties in low self-esteem?

- Low self-esteem may lead to a variety of problems, including the following:
- Please, please, please, please, please, please, please
- Anger or irritation readily sets in. You think your viewpoint isn't significant
- It's never good enough to do what you've done.
- As a result, you're very sensitive to the views of others.
- The world doesn't feel secure at the moment.
- You question every choice you make.
- Sadness and a sense of inadequacy are feelings you often feel.
- You have difficulty maintaining close personal connections. You shy away from taking chances or attempting novel experiences.

- As a result of your compulsive attempts to avoid situations, you have developed an addiction to
- Your self-esteem is a constant source of concern for you.
- It's tough for you to set limits.
- You focus more on your flaws than you do on your strengths.
- You can't say no or ask for what you want because you're afraid. You're unclear about who you are.
- When your view on life is gloomy, you distrust your own skills and your prospects of achievement.
- Fear, anxiety, and despair are some of the most common unpleasant feelings you deal with on a regular basis.
- When you measure yourself against others, you're typically left feeling underwhelmed.

Self-Esteem Statistics and Facts You've Never Heard of Before

Self-esteem and the reasons for its importance might be difficult to comprehend. Some of the most important and relevant results regarding self-esteem, particularly low self-esteem, have been collected for your benefit.

Some of these statistics may seem obvious to you, but you may be surprised to learn just how widespread and pervasive low self-esteem is among the general population (and particularly young people and girls).

These are the details:

- Teenage males who have strong self-esteem are roughly 2.5 times more likely than those who have low self-esteem to initiate sexual contact. In contrast, females who have high self-esteem are three times as likely as those who have poor self-esteem to delay having sex..
- Violent behaviour, school dropouts and adolescent pregnancies are all connected to poor self-esteem.
- High school students are trying to shed pounds at an alarming rate: 44 per cent of females and 15 per cent of guys.
- Girls think that they aren't good enough or don't measure up in some manner, according to 7 out of 10 of them.

- When it comes to a girl's self-esteem, her body image is more important than her actual weight.
- The majority of females (almost 90%) want to alter some element of their looks.
- In fact, 81% of 10-year-old girls are frightened of getting overweight.
- An eating problem affects around one in four college-aged women.
- Only 2% of females believe in their own beauty.

Self-esteem is negatively impacted by the absence of dads, poverty, and a squalid family environment.

They may be shocking and depressing, but they are not the complete picture when it comes to self-esteem. Self-esteem has numerous benefits and advantages, and this narrative indicates that many individuals have a good feeling of self-esteem. For example, those with a strong sense of self-worth:

- Reduce their self- and other-criticism.
- Improved stress management and reduced risk of stress-related health problems.
- Possess a lower risk of developing anorexia.

- Do not suffer from feelings of self-loathing or humiliation.
- Do a better job of communicating and obtaining their desires.
- They are more inclined to exit bad relationships and create solid, honest ones.
- That they are confident in their ability to make the correct decisions.
- Possess a greater capacity for rebounding from disappointment, failure, and other setbacks.
- A look into how self-esteem might be developed is clearly important given the current status of self-esteem and its good effects on people's lives.

Self-Esteem Boosting Strategies You Can Use Today

Do a self-assessment to get a sense of where you are.

It's as easy as making a list of 10 things you're good at and ten things you're bad at. Start by building an honest and realistic view of yourself with the aid of this guideline.

Make certain that your expectations are grounded in reality.

Small, attainable objectives are critical to your success. For example, if you set unrealistic expectations for yourself or expect someone else to modify their behaviour, you will almost certainly feel like a failure because of it.

Stop trying to be flawless.

Acknowledge your successes and failures, and don't be afraid to admit them. Trying to be flawless can only lead to disappointment, and no one is. In order to have a good view and develop from your errors, it is important to acknowledge your achievements as well as your failures.

The fourth phase is to become acquainted with oneself.

Self-awareness and self-acceptance are critical life skills that cannot be understated. While it may take some time and effort, the trip is one that should be conducted with a sense of purpose and enthusiasm.

Be open to the possibility of altering your self-perception.

Keeping up with our ever-evolving selves is essential if we wish to create and attain meaningful objectives.

Never compare one's own achievements with those of others.

It's simpler than ever to compare ourselves to others because of the growth of social media and its ability to create a beautifully polished picture. The only person to whom you should hold a mirror up is yourself.

Put an end to your inner critic by saying, "Stop!" to it.

Motivate yourself in a more healthy way.

You deserve a two-minute moment of self-appreciation.

In the evening, make a list of three positive aspects of your personality that you are grateful for.

Do what is right.

- Let go of your need for perfection.
- When things go wrong, focus on the good aspects of the experience rather than the negative.
- Be more considerate of other people's feelings.
- Take a chance on something different.
- Stop comparing yourself to others.

- Get to know more uplifting individuals (and less time with destructive people).
- Keep in mind the "whys" of having a strong sense of self-worth.

Counseling and Therapy

Do we have the ability to help people improve their self-esteem via therapy and counseling?

There are various ways therapy and counseling may help individuals enhance their self-esteem, as shown by studies like those discussed above.

For those with poor self-esteem, counseling may be an effective way to boost their confidence.

Therapy and counseling may help a client's self-esteem in the following ways:

Self-esteem may be built on the basis of acceptance and compassion rather than criticism or correction when a client expresses their inner thoughts and emotions to a professional therapist.

Clients who have been treated in this way for a long period of time begin to think, "Maybe there's nothing wrong with me after all!"

This can help the client realise that he could be exactly the same person but have high self-esteem instead of low self-esteem; the therapist should explain to him how self-esteem is a belief and that our beliefs are based on our experiences; this can help the client realise that his current level of self-esteem could be replaced with one of high self-esteem instead of low self-esteem; of high self-esteem.

New experiences for the therapist might help the client form a new belief about herself, one that is "essentially acceptable" rather than "basically bad." Clients might learn to accept themselves by seeing their therapist accept them.

Rather of condemning the client, the therapist should be able to accept him as he is and confirm his views and emotions as valid. Clients' self-esteem is greatly enhanced when their therapist accepts and approves of who they are on a fundamental level, regardless of whether or not they take every action the client does.

By following these rules, you may help your client build a greater sense of self-love and self-worth. You can also discourage "needless shame" and help her learn to detach herself from her conduct by following these instructions.

The Advantages of Meditating to Improve One's Self-Esteem

There are several ways to increase one's self-esteem than relying just on medical treatment.

Meditation is one of various methods for improving one's mental health, and it is recommended by many experts.On the other hand, Meditation has a number of additional advantages beyond just improving our sense of self-worth.

Let go, and perspective are two skills that we learn via meditation. Our minds are trained to just watch rather than actively engage in every single event that comes into our minds. As a result, we're "loosening the hold we have on our sense of ourselves".

Developing and sustaining a good self-image may seem counterintuitive, yet this is an effective strategy. A key benefit of meditation is that it enables us to become more aware of our inner sensations without being emotionally invested in them.

The tendency to over-identify with one's self might explain low self-esteem. A concentration on the positive (I am the best) or negative (I am the worst) might cause us to put an excessive amount of significance on it. Every phrase, idea, and sensation that comes into our minds might become compulsive for us.

Daily meditation practice may help liberate you from being governed by the ideas and sensations you encounter in your own mind to raise your self-esteem.

An excessively critical inner voice is less powerful when you are able to stand back and notice troubling or self-deprecating thoughts; this identification with the negative ideas you have about yourself leads to less negative discourse over time.

Summing up:

It is critical to note the following: Self-confidence is defined as a sense of faith in one's own talents and the idea that one has the necessary resources to meet any challenge that may come your way. When you are self-assured, you put your confidence and faith in yourself as well as in the future.

It provides you with a strong feeling of control over your life since you are aware of your own strengths and understands that you have the ability to positively affect every event that occurs in your life.However, even if circumstances are beyond your control, if you have self-confidence in your talents and know that you will make the most of any situation, you will feel more at ease in your own skin.

In terms of self-esteem and self-worth, it is more important to consider how you regard yourself as a person rather than how you compare yourself to others. There is a connection between this and self-confidence since when you respect yourself, you are more likely to feel confident in your abilities. As a result, you may utilise these positive affirmations for low self-esteem to help you feel better about yourself.

Currently, we are living in an era characterized by high levels of stress. When you add in unanticipated occurrences, such as the public health catastrophe we're now dealing with as a result of the coronavirus, our anxiety becomes even more heightened.

In order to avoid feeling overwhelmed when confined at home during the pandemic, the good news is that there are simple steps you can take to keep your anxiety under control while you're in quarantine at home.

The concepts of self-respect and self-esteem have been thoroughly discussed in this chapter, and you should now have the knowledge to distinguish between the two and take the necessary steps to cultivate each of them.

Chapter:3

How COVID Pandemic Effect Self Esteem Or Self Improvement

The coronavirus pandemic is a public health and psychological emergency. The immensity of living in solitude, the changes that occur in our everyday lives, such as job loss, financial struggle, and sadness over the death of a loved one, all have the potential to negatively impact the mental health and well-being of many people.

However, even in the midst of physical separation, it is vital to seek out social support and to maintain connections with others. In addition, it is critical to understand the indicators of anxiety, panic attacks, depression, and suicide so that you can recognize them in others, including family, friends, and neighbors, as well as in yourself, when you are experiencing these feelings.

The latest epidemic has had severe consequences around the world, since its appearance and spread have caused bewilderment, worry, and dread among the general populace. The outbreak of a pandemic makes an already tough situation considerably more difficult. There is a high danger of acquiring mental health problems as a result of the pandemic; in fact, mental illnesses related with unanticipated outbreaks have been reported in over half of unaffected populations throughout the world. Several studies have found that mental health issues can develop in healthcare professionals and pandemic survivors during a pandemic outbreak. Mental health services are responding to the issue by providing online, outpatient, and inpatient mental health treatments to all of the areas who require them. International organizations such as the World Health Organization (WHO) acknowledge the importance of mental health in attaining overall health, and mental health has been included into population health initiatives by a number of different jurisdictions. There is some evidence that a negative psychological attribute, such as poor self-esteem, may have a role in the development of mental health disorders.

Low self-esteem is not often recognized as a mental health problem, yet it is strongly associated with poor mental health. Self-esteem is considered to be a very consistent aspect of one's personality, yet it might change as a result of disappointments or recent triumphs, according to research. Self-esteem is defined as the beliefs that a person has about himself, which can be positive or negative, good or terrible, correct or wrong.

Persons with low self-esteem, according to Campbell, regarded themselves as less remarkable, less confidential, less fast, and with less temporal stability than individuals with high self-esteem did. Depression is compounded by poor self-esteem, which is a contributing cause. A higher elevated feeling of self-esteem has been recognized as one of the personal attributes that contributes to psychological outcomes that are more resistant to stress. Low self-esteem, on the other hand, may be a risk factor for developing negative psychological repercussions. Self-esteem may serve as a predictor of how well a person would cope with and handle psychological issues, which in turn may have an impact on one's mental health and level of life satisfaction.

When it comes to measuring life satisfaction, it is used as a primary construct that is related to other emotional, social, and behavioral constructs. One variable that may have an influence on life satisfaction is self-esteem. In contrast to self-esteem, life satisfaction is defined as an individual's overall rating of his or her life, which covers many aspects of his or her life, such as school, family, and friends, in addition to one's or her own judgments and assessments of oneself. According to Frisch's research, an individual's level of life satisfaction is determined by the extent to which positive emotions outnumber negative emotions in their lives. According to the World Health Organization, life satisfaction is a subjective measure of overall well-being that is based on people's views of their contentment or enjoyment with their lives in general.

Self-esteem has been connected with a number of social, behavioral, and developmental aspects, which have been discovered in the research. Having a pleasant sense of well-being is another strong predictor of good physical and mental health outcomes that is connected with peak performance. The quality of one's life, as judged by contentment with one's self, family, friends, and school environment, is linked to a young person's self-rated mental health, according to one research.

There have been very few studies conducted on psychological traits such as mental health, self-esteem, and life satisfaction in the general population that have made comparisons across gender, geographic region, and occupational classification. I believe that more research should beThis is an area in which I feel additional study should be conducted.As a result, the major goal of this study is to explore how different types of individuals living in Ethiopia may differ in terms of their mental health, self-esteem, and level of contentment with their lives. In addition, the proportional contribution of mental health to self-esteem and life happiness is determined by this research.

Simply said, one percent would result in an immense improvement for all of the constituents of that society, including both physical individuals and the institutions and environment in which this society runs. It's that easy. An upheaval of social identities, routines, and obligations is a situation characterized by the disturbance of social roles.Since the COVID-19 virus pandemic has spread, people's everyday lives have been thrown into disarray, putting their health and safety at risk as well as the social roles that keep them functioning.. For example, parents educating their children, friends interacting online, and employees working from home are all part of our collective effort to tackle the infection. While these communal efforts are beneficial to the greater good, people's social positions are no longer consistent with what they were before to the outbreak of the pandemic in the first place.Many people's mental health may be negatively affected by this.. As a result, people lose touch with their "true" selves and lose their sense of belonging in social situations. As proof, we present survey and experimental findings that COVID-19-related role shifts do, in fact, promote inauthenticity in the workplace. People's feelings about COVID-19 and their feelings about the role transition had no influence on this outcome, in addition, we discover two moderators of this impact in the literature. In the first instance, this impact happens when (and allegedly because) the social roles that are changing are fundamental to an individual's sense of self Second, the duration of this impact is dependent on the individual's temporal viewpoint.As long as individuals keep their attention on the present and the near future rather than the past or the distant future, shifting social positions do not have to entail losing one's true self (post-COVID-19).This benefit for present-focused coping has been demonstrated in both the United States and Hong Kong. We propose that people feel more truly themselves when they keep a present focus is because doing so reduces the salience of the gap between their social roles.

Personal growth is always discussed from the perspective of the individual, but now I want to elevate it to a higher level, to the level of the social community. In which case, theoretically, we all profit.

After reading about persons who aim to improve themselves by one percent on a daily basis, I came to believe that after a hundred days, they would have become a person who was 100 percent better, or twice as excellent as they were before. As a result of considering if this is a reasonable notion, I have come to the conclusion that it is not, and the explanation has a little amount of logic.

Every day may provide a fresh opportunity to learn something new or to establish new habits, but we will never be able to change even a tenth of our personality in a single 24-hour period.

Think about everything you are, including your knowledge and connections as well as your actions and routines, as well as your stuff and everything else that has an impact on who you are in some way or another.We have a great deal of knowledge in our heads, and everything around us is essentially incalculable in terms of quantity. It is not feasible to make even a tenth of a percent of these changes in a single day.

Hopefully, I will be able to complete this in a year, and only if I put out a superhuman effort in the process.

As a result, one method to get closer to the feasible would be for each generation to make slight improvements to themselves. It is sufficient if the evolution occurs at a rate of 0.5 percent during the mature period. The quality of life for the next generation would greatly increase as a consequence of this.

Let me now elaborate on what transpired leading up to this incidence. As previously said, each individual must make a one-percent improvement over a certain length of time, and in order to do so, he must put into practice specific behaviors that increase his overall well-being.

People's sense of self is fundamentally influenced by their social positions. As a result, we identify ourselves in terms of our social positions.On the other hand, our social roles evolve in lockstep with our surroundings.Change is being triggered on a worldwide scale by the recent coronavirus (COVID-19) pandemic, and joint attempts to contain its spread have resulted in significant and unprecedented changes to societal structures and roles. COVID-19 cases are on the rise, society is in flux, and 60% of the world's population will be restricted from travelling by August 2021, according to the United Nations Population Division. The meantime, as the virus spreads around the globe, different communities are experiencing new and resurgent disturbances. Due to the unprecedented increase in the number of daily new cases that occurred beginning in late April, the Indian government instituted a new round of strict regional lockdowns, and the Australian government has been renewing regional lockdowns throughout the summer months as well.

Although collective effort to halt the spread of the pandemic is vital, the lives of individuals who work within these social structures are upended as a result of the outbreak. The same person who was previously juggling multiple social roles (such as that of a parent, employee, and friend) may now be faced with new responsibilities The suspension of all social roles, for example, homeschooling children, behavioural patterns (such as working in the office while wearing a mask), or even the execution of duties in settings outside than the workplace (such as chatting online) (e.g., furloughed employment). It is notable that social role modifications under COVID-19 are detrimental to people's interpersonal connections and psychological well-being because of the danger they bring to them. Parenting during lockdowns, for example, can exacerbate parent-child conflict while also causing emotional strain, stress, and burnout in the parent. Because of the enormous emotional-cognitive demands and challenges to their professional skills, healthcare employees feel psychological anguish and a "breaking" of their social identities in the job. As with any other group of students, student athletes who are denied the opportunity to participate in team sports and activities face social identity threats as well as decreased well-being and increased depression symptoms. To summarize, the collective activities that cultures are doing to tackle COVID-19 are disturbing societal roles in a way that causes social and psychological distress among the general population.

A person's sense of self-authenticity—the conviction that one's thoughts, emotions, and actions are in accordance with one's own identity on a personal level—is the focus of the present research. While self-authenticity is a critical facet of mental health that should not be disregarded even in the best of circumstances, it becomes much more critical under COVID-19. When it comes to mental health, self-authenticity is seen as the cornerstone, having been defined as "not only a facet or precursor to wellbeing, but rather the fundamental core of wellbeing and well-functioning." As a result, preserving authenticity entails preserving mental health in a more general sense. Indeed, inauthenticity is connected with (but separate from) lower self-esteem as well as higher stress, anxiety, and depression, as well as unhappiness in romantic relationships and unethical activity. It is also crucial to protect authenticity since state inauthenticity can grow into chronic inauthenticity over time, which is dangerous. COVID-19-related role alterations may therefore have long-lasting impacts on the self, even long after the pandemic has ended, if otherwise transient experiences of inauthenticity become the new normal for an individual.

Furthermore, the perspective of self-authenticity provides a fresh approach to developing coping mechanisms to increase psychological well-being in the context of COVID-19. It has been discovered that when people sense self-continuity, or the constancy of their identity across time, they feel more real. Our study suggests that COVID-19-related role shifts promote inauthenticity by diminishing the continuity of the self over time, and we utilize this thesis to examine coping techniques for COVID-19 that differ in their temporal perspective (i.e., past, present, or future). The findings add to studies on dealing with COVID-19, and as such, they are both substantively valuable and timely in their publication. Indeed, there is emerging research that links emotional well-being during COVID-19 to temporal views, which is now under investigation. It is possible, according to this research, that one's temporal perspective impacts one's health during COVID-19; however, it does not pit different temporal perspectives against one another, nor does it address dealing with challenges to one's own authenticity. As a result of this inquiry, new knowledge about self-authenticity has been added to the body of knowledge. Self-inauthenticity has been linked to social role disruption, which has been recognized as a precursor. Furthermore, we demonstrate that previously identified techniques for coping with inauthenticity (e.g., nostalgia, looking backward) are less effective during this current epidemic.

Disruption of social roles and a sense of self-authenticity

In social structure, social roles are defined as "positions in the structure that carry societal expectations for the conduct of those who occupy them." These can include, for example, the positions of kid, parent, friend, love partner, or employee, to name a few possibilities.There is a possibility that people's self-perception may be influenced by the roles they play and how they feel about themselves. People's real feelings might be influenced by their social roles, in particular. If a person performs a social role in a way that is not true to themselves (for example, by putting their own needs second in a love relationship), they will feel unauthentic in their performance. People also feel unauthentic if they believe there is little integration between social roles or if they assume a large number of distinct social roles. On the basis of this research, we propose that social role disturbances, such as those connected with the COVID-19 epidemic, can also cause people to feel untrue to themselves. Authenticity, we hypothesize, is undermined by such interruptions because they cause self-continuity to be reduced.

An individual's subjective perception that their past, present, and future selves are all connected is known as "self-continuity" in psychology.People who have a steady autobiographical story across time will subjectively perceive self-continuity and will feel that they are being true to themselves. People, on the other hand, who have an autobiography that lacks temporal coherence would feel unauthentic. Previous study has discovered that transitioning from one life position to another destabilizes one's sense of self. Specific to this, the disruption of a significant life function results in liminality, a situation in which personal identities are suspended, self-concept becomes uncertain, and self-continuity is decreased. In light of this, consider how the breadth and scope of social role disruptions under COVID-19 may have an influence on a person's capacity to keep his or her own personal identity. As previously stated, the obligations, routines, and situations that are crucial to social roles are changing, with certain social roles being completely suspended. So COVID-19 disrupts the temporal continuity that underpins social roles; its severe disturbances to the rhythm of everyday life render time practically "meaningless," whereby the "old normal" has been replaced by a "new normal," but the "new normal" has not yet been attained. People's sense of inauthenticity is likely to be heightened as a result of social role disruptions since the methods un which they practice these roles lack continuity from what they considered to be authentic to these roles before to COVID-19.

It is crucial to emphasize that "disruptions" in social roles that occur as a result of COVID-19 are not always detrimental. People may interpret role changes (for example, homeschooling children) either adversely (for example, losing childcare) or favorably (for example, learning new skills) (e.g., spending more time with family). Inauthenticity has been linked to both negative and positive actions, such as cheating and using luxury brands, in previous research. So we propose that people's perceptions of role change under COVID-19, and more broadly of the law COVID-19 in general, are conceptually and empirically separate from the amount to which role change occurs under COVID-19 and the influence of role change on inauthenticity.The extent to which COVID-19 has changed people's social roles is predicted to cause them to feel inauthentic, and this is predicted to occur regardless of (i.e., statistically controlling for) how positively or negatively they feel about COVID-19 or about the role change itself, as demonstrated in the studies.

Low self-esteem caused by society

Society has very bad effects if taken negatively, individuality is purportedly encouraged in today's culture, yet people are still discriminated against and assessed based on their appearance, behavior, and emotions. Because they are growing up and finding who they are, teens are constantly exposed to negative influences in the world around them.

'I think it's very sad that we have so many false pictures impacting our perceptions of what we consider to be attractive and what we consider to be not,' Paige Savarese, a freshman, said. It is important for people to understand that what they see on a billboard, the cover of a magazine, and in a movie is a depiction of the top one percent of the population who have had a team of professionals work together to make them appear that way. "It's completely impractical and absurd."

Seeing all of these photos of the most gorgeous and acceptable individuals has a negative impact on how people, particularly teenagers, perceive themselves and can lead to low self-esteem difficulties. Society is all around us. We are talking about the folks in our classroom, our family at home, and complete strangers on the street. It's the passage of our life as they pass us by. It encompasses everything that has ever existed. The fact that it is a monster is the most significant thing. People strive to be what society considers to be "beautiful," but the truth is that genuine beauty can only be found within. It is society's conception of beauty that causes many people to have poor self-esteem and negative self-images when they might be more positive and confident about their own appearances.

Girls aspire to be like Barbie, who has the beautiful form and lives the perfect life, among other things. Self-esteem is a mental condition in which an individual perceives oneself or herself to be inadequate, undeserving of affection, unworthy of success, and/or unable of doing basic tasks. Once created, a negative self-image pervades every thought, resulting in erroneous assumptions and a pattern of self-defeating behavior that continues indefinitely. Teens and young adults, particularly those in high school, frequently struggle with low self-esteem difficulties. Seven out of ten females think that they are not good enough or that they do not measure up in some manner, whether it is in terms of their appearance, academic achievement, or relationships with friends and family members Teenage females are more than twice as likely than teenage boys to have a low sense of self-worth as they are. Physical attractiveness, according to a study conducted by the American Association of University Women, was shown to be the most important indication of one's sense of self-worth. Boys, on the other hand, valued their self-worth in terms of their capacity to do tasks. Girls are more concerned with how they seem, such as if their hair is straight enough and whether their makeup is not smeared. 'If it isn't good enough for them, it isn't good enough for anyone else,' they believe.Many men are concerned with their appearance as well, but their primary concern is whether or not they are capable of doing what their buddies are capable of.

Even an adult's self-esteem can be affected by the social pressures that they are subjected to. A person's life continues to be influenced by the media, regardless of their age.According to Dove, 80 percent of adult women are concerned about their own beauty because of images of other women on television and in movies. The pattern was established throughout their teens. Men are still more likely than women to feel a strong sense of self-worth, but as adults, they are under increased pressure to take the initiative. Men who have a family and a career are more likely than those who do not to have a good sense of self-esteem.

Teens may find it difficult to recognize their own attractiveness when the media portrays them as having model bodies and telling them that this is what being beautiful looks like, according to experts. The pursuit of an unachievable beauty should not cause someone to feel scrutinized and self-conscious about their appearance. Humans are all unique, and no two people are alike; nevertheless, today's culture is focused on conformity and social acceptability rather than individuality.

I firmly believe that individuals should be proud of who they are and ignore all of the society expectations on how they should appear in order to be happy. Nothing more than being the greatest version of yourself and being content with that is anything you can ask of yourself. No one should be expected to look same because we are all individuals with unique characteristics.

Despite the fact that the majority of people are more aware of poor self-esteem issues linked with girls, guys are also influenced by social standards.

More than 40% of males in middle school and high school frequently exercise with the purpose of growing muscle mass, and 38% use protein supplements, according to a recent survey of the population. A further 6 percent of respondents acknowledged to experimenting with anabolic steroids.

To think that we would inject hazardous drugs into our bodies and engage in bad practices in order to conform is alarming. Instead, we should embrace ourselves for who we are, including our physical appearance, and learn to love ourselves for who we are.

Self-esteem is important, and as individuals, we should be confident in our own skin and our own appearance, irrespective of the effect of the media and the wider society on our lives. Adolescence is commonly acknowledged to be one of the most rapid periods of growth and development a person can go through. This condition is characterized by fast development in physical, social, and cognitive abilities, as well as significant changes in self-esteem. Several studies have found that one's self-esteem has a considerable influence on crucial life outcomes, such as health and social outcomes, during adolescence and early adulthood. Increased self-esteem, for example, is clearly associated with positive outcomes such as vocational success, improved social connections, a sense of well-being, and favourable evaluations by peers, as well as greater levels of academic accomplishment and effective coping abilities. Depression, drug misuse, antisocial behavior, and suicide are all linked to low self-esteem in one way or another. Children with poor self-esteem have lower social functioning, as seen by their reduced acceptability by their peers, according to the research.

Extensive study has been conducted to identify risk and protective variables associated with the development of low self-esteem throughout adolescence.Risk factors for teen pregnancy and pregnancy-related mortality include a girl's academic performance and grades, her family's socioeconomic situation and parental education, the availability of free or reduced-price school meals, the parents' work status, and obesity.

Academic accomplishment has been shown to be influenced by self-esteem, and academic achievement has been shown to be influenced by self-esteem. The ability to have high self-esteem has been identified as an essential predictor of kids' academic accomplishment. Another study discovered that while high self-esteem was associated with a variety of favorable outcomes and advantages, it was not always associated with high academic achievement. Adolescents with poor academic performance, on the other hand, were not necessarily associated with low general self-esteem.

A lack of self-esteem can be linked to a variety of behavioural and mental health difficulties, such as drug abuse, early sex, and eating disorders, among others. Teenage eating and other unhealthy behaviours have been linked to low self-esteem, but not drug use or early sexual activity, according to a large sample of young New Zealanders studied over a lengthy period of time. Among terms of mental health, researchers have discovered a link between poor self-esteem, sadness, and anxiety, as well as suicide ideation and attempts in teenagers.

Academic pressure has been linked to a variety of negative emotions, including stress, sadness, anxiety, and low self-esteem in students in secondary or high school, as well as in young people (23–25), according to research published in the last few years."Studying or thinking too much," according to the findings of a study in Hue, Vietnam, contributes to mental health problems (26). In Vietnamese culture, it is reasonable to predict that the pressure from parents and schools will have an unexpected consequence, resulting in decreased self-esteem and the accompanying effects that have been observed elsewhere among high school students.Only a few descriptive or analytical research have been done in Vietnam on the issue of teenage self-esteem, and there have been no systematic investigations.

In light of our findings, this is especially pertinent because we identified high levels of depression and suicide thoughts among Vietnamese high school students. When it comes to the prevalence of low self-esteem, as well as the characteristics associated with low self-esteem and the relationships between low self-esteem and the like, a study of secondary school pupils has been done according to this article.We hypothesized that having low self-esteem would be related with a higher likelihood of having poor mental health status in the long run.

Society and its effect on self-improvement

Many, if not most, of the main issues affecting society today have their roots in poor self-esteem among many of the individuals who make up society, according to a more specific notion that underpins our endeavor here. Individuals who value themselves and have a sense of personal empowerment, it is assumed, will nurture their own personal responsibility and will attention to the duties that are essential for the well-being of their communities and the general welfare of the society. This year's unique coronavirus illness (COVID-19) pandemic, which began in March, has presented a substantial danger to the global health system on a global scale. According to the United Nations' assessment, "while the COVID-19 situation is, in the first instance, a physical health catastrophe, it has the potential to develop into a significant mental health crisis if nothing is done" (United Nations 2020).

The COVID-19 epidemic and subsequent quarantine have been connected to anxiety, sadness, stress, post-traumatic stress disorder (PTSD), and poor sleep, according to a number of study publications. Furthermore, it has been proposed that the pandemic may have a major influence on the risk and symptoms of eating disorders. Also assumed is that people in society who are burdened with the feeling that they are unworthy would seek shelter in activities that are unproductive, expensive, deviant and hazardous to society and will thus contribute disproportionately to major societal issues as a result of their beliefs. Due to the importance placed on these two propositions, it becomes necessary for the leaders of society to first establish social conditions that will maximize the development of self-esteem among the population; and second, to establish social arrangements that will rescue and rehabilitate those who have emerged from their families and communities with a diminished sense of self-worth. That is the mission of the California Task Force to Promote Self-Esteem, and it is the agenda that we are putting to the best critical test possible in this special book on self-esteem and social problems in light of the finest social scientific research now accessible to us.

In light of our findings, this is especially pertinent because we identified high levels of depression and suicide thoughts among Vietnamese high school students. When it comes to the prevalence of low self-esteem, as well as the characteristics associated with low self-esteem and the relationships between low self-esteem and the like, a stWhat Does It Mean to Have a High Sense of Self-Esteem?udy of secondary school pupils has been done according to this article.

Approximately two years ago, two of my theoretically oriented colleagues in West Germany embarked on a big research project that is still ongoing. It was on the subject of "the key social issues in postmodern Western culture," according to the report. After two years of hard labor, they came to the following conclusion: "We have been able to identify that we cannot describe nor quantify either 'major social crises' or 'postmodern Western civilization.' That brings our study report to a close." However, it has been discovered, and this has been stated by the contributors to this volume, that we confront a number of conceptual difficulties when attempting to understand the nature of self-esteem and the different behavioral implications that result from it in the first place.

As previously said, we have a reasonably good understanding of what it means to have high self-esteem, as indicated by our own introspection and observation of the conduct of others, among other things. However, it is difficult to express that knowledge in precise terms. When we try to describe something, we are unsure about, we often fumble around with a lot of different terms, none of which catches the core of what we are trying to convey. In addition to self-esteem, our writers have recognized the concepts of self, self-concept, self-respect, awareness, identity, image, congruence, and consciousness as well as other related concepts such as self-esteem. None of them are very successful, though.. No less true are the negative opposites, such as a lack of self-concept, impotence, helplessness, ineffectiveness, inefficacy, self-derogation, anxiety-induced sadness, or a loss of self-esteem. Does this definitional labyrinth hold any useful information for us at this point? How much of this definitional quagmire can be salvaged?

One place to begin is by identifying the components of the notion that are virtually generally recognized as being true. First and foremost, there is a cognitive component; self-esteem is defined as the ability to characterize certain aspects of one's self in descriptive words, such as power, confidence, and action. It entails inquiring as to what sort of person one is. Second, there is an emotional component, a valence or degree of positiveness or negativizes associated with the characteristics that have been found; this is referred to as high or low self-esteem, respectively. Third, and closely connected to the second, there is an evaluative aspect, which is the assigning of a level of merit to something in accordance with an idealized norm.

Another characteristic of self-esteem is the existence of a standard. Sometimes the benchmark is a person's absolute sense of self-worth, which is judged against an ego ideal that one has set for himself or herself. In other words, it might be considered a relative standard, assessing one's feeling of self-worth in comparison to an internal aim or desired degree of achievement. It is possible that the standard or point of reference is mostly internal or psychological in nature; yet, it is also possible that one's self-worth is measured in relation to another individual or group. Members of minority groups, who compare their own group's fortunes to the fortunes of other groups in society, are particularly concerned about the latter instance, which is particularly relevant.

When we analyze the stability of the idea of self-esteem, definitional challenges become much more difficult to resolve. It is appropriate to consider it to be some sort of global attribute, one that maintains a consistent degree of strength and organization for the individual. Or should it be viewed as primarily a situational phenomenon? Each of us is familiar with the fact that we may feel good about ourselves one minute and horrible about ourselves the next, depending on our mood and social setting. The fact that high self-esteem can be perceived as an intrinsic set of sentiments at times, but can also be seen as a defensive reaction to feelings of inferiority or inadequacy, further complicates the situation. A strong sense of self-worth is more accurately defined as vanity, hubris, or egotism in the latter case. All of these definitional obstacles will be brought into play when we address problems of measurement or when we attempt to arrive at operational definitions of the notion in question.

Theoretically, we are somewhat better off in terms of the alleged behavioral repercussions of high or low self-esteem than we are in terms of actual conduct, but not by much. Definitions are most simply defined in regions where their opposites are clearly distinguished from one another on the basis of their behavioral characteristics. It is easier to recognize when someone isn't learning because of the institutional nature of their relationship to school, but it is more difficult to recognize when someone isn't doing well in school. When someone is out of work, it is generally simple to determine; nevertheless, the phenomena of part-time work, seeking or not seeking employment, and unpaid labor all complicate this determination further. It is quite simple to characterize teenage sexual activity, and it is also pretty simple to define teenage pregnancy in the United States. It is simple to specify what we mean by ingestion of a certain chemical ingredient; nevertheless, it is far more difficult to explain what we mean by ingestion of "too much." We have a good understanding of what we mean by "crime," but we struggle to come up with a precise description of what constitutes "violence." The most difficult issues to deal with are those involving child maltreatment. They utilize legal, medical, sexual, and psychological definitions of the term, each of which has an own set of implications.

It is particularly crucial to emphasize these definitional issues because we want to ensure that definitions of alleged causes (for example, poor self-esteem) are maintained apart from definitions of alleged behavioral effects (for example, substance abuse) (e.g., psychological stimulation by drugs or alcohol). Otherwise, we will be caught identifying the same things twice, which will make it difficult to explain that they are distinct from one another and impossible to avoid circular reasoning in our thinking.

The influence of social life and its consequences

Has the question, "What is social change?" ever crossed your mind? You've undoubtedly heard the word tossed about before, and you may have even learnt a little bit about it in school at some point. One way or another, the concept of social transformation can be defined.However, as humans who live in this world, knowing social change and how it has played a part in our lives throughout history will enable us to promote social change both now and, in the future,, which will benefit all of us.

To what extent should we be concerned about social change?

Socioeconomic change has a profound effect on human interactions, relationships, behaviour patterns, and cultural standards. Social change can be measured in terms of percentage changes in population. These transformations eventually result in the transformation of cultural and social institutions, conceptions, and regulations, which will unavoidably have a long-term influence on society. These transformations and alterations are not always positive or negative, but they are significant nonetheless. The effects of social change might be subtle at first glance; yet, it can take years, and in some cases, centuries, of work to bring about a significant shift.

Students and citizens of a quickly changing society must take the time to reflect on societal developments that have occurred in the past and how they have impacted our current situation. Examples include the fact that women were not previously authorised to seek higher education at one point in time.. Today, men and women of all colors, faiths, nations, and creeds can pursue higher education — even online and tuition-free programs like those offered by the University of the People. Because of this, social transformation is very important. We can only move forward as a community if we implement social change.

Interactions with others are the starting point for change.

We begin by deciding how and when we will interact with one another. Change is propelled by a variety of factors including ideological, political, and economic movements to name a few.. Social change is typically initiated at the grassroots level and progresses upward, first affecting society as a whole, then legislators and those in positions of authority.

However, it is possible for it to shift from the top down, like when a new leader takes over as president. For us to effect change, we must be open to hearing other people's perspectives and engaging in sometimes painful dialogues with those who disagree with us. It's about taking the time to hear another person's point of view on a particular problem, even if you don't exactly agree with them. Furthermore, it is important to be persistent and to fight for what you believe in, even if it is challenging at times.

The Continually Shifting Social Order

Taking a theoretical approach to social change, the next step is to comprehend the shifting social order, which is one of the most comprehensive approaches to comprehending social change. No matter how much social change occurs all the time, it is important to understand that there are two kinds of social change: changes within the social system (which help to keep the system in place) and changes that have the potential to completely alter that system, which are referred to as "societal changes."

There are a variety of alternative classifications for social change that may be used. It is possible for social change to occur on a local scale, but this does not always translate into significant changes in the larger society. For example, shifting conditions inside a tribal entity, but not within the broader government in which the tribe is based, are instances of this phenomenon. For example, a small village may decide to adopt a more environmentally friendly lifestyle, such as collectively recycling plastic and picking up rubbish, despite the fact that the region in which they reside may not have any laws requiring them to do so or has not set any precedents in this regard.

It is also possible to categorize social change according to whether it occurred over a short period of time or over a longer length of time.

Only humans are endowed with the faculties necessary to effect societal change. As a result of our biology, as well as our capacity to adapt, learn, and be adaptable — especially as our environment changes around us — we have the power to continuously inspire social change, regardless of whether or not we are the ones who begin it. As a result, the social order is shifting.

Chapter 4

Too late before the problem manifest

What is self-esteem? Taking care of oneself is the key. Taking care of one's own needs is the key.Taking good care of one's bodily and mental well-being is a sign of high self-esteem. "The acts that people do for themselves, on behalf of and alongside others in order to develop, protect, maintain and enhance their health, wellbeing or wellness," is how the Self Care Forum defines self-esteem in the UK. According to the Royal Australasian College of Physicians, self-esteem comprises 'taking after your needs, on a daily basis and in times of crisis, to preserve a healthy emotional, psychological and physiological resilience'

In order to practise self-esteem, you must be self-aware and connected; you must know what to do and what not to do in order to maintain your health. It is the ability to take responsibility of your own mental, emotional, and physical well-being that is called self-awareness. It's the realization that your well-being, happiness, and health may suffer if you don't take care of yourself.

A one-time event, self-esteem is a daily practise that must be continued.Health and wellness is an ongoing journey. A portion of who you are is the things that you do every day.

"Our objective is to integrate it (self-esteem) into everyone's daily life and make it a lifelong habit and culture," Dr. Pete Smith, co-chair of Self Care Forum, stated in 2018 about Self Care Week, an annual UK national awareness week.

It is our goal that everyone has a basic understanding of how to take care of their own bodily and psychological well-being. A better, healthier, and more satisfying existence can only be achieved through self-esteem.'

Becoming aware of your own needs is the first step in determining how much self-esteem you require at any given moment. To put it another way, if you're feeling a little overwhelmed right now, self-esteem can entail finding strategies to deal with this time in your life. Slowing down, resting, and reflecting may be necessary. In order to improve your quality of life, you may want to engage in activities that allow you to connect with people and the environment around you.

Acute or chronic disease or disability may necessitate self-esteem for certain persons.Finding a work-life balance that works for you may be an issue for others. It might mean getting more exercise or eating a more nutritious diet. A daily stroll, journaling, or reading a book could be examples of self-esteem for some of us. For others, self-esteem may include any number of other activities. For example, you may sign up for a dancing class or take a motorcycle driving course. Everything that makes you feel better both physically and emotionally is part of self-esteem.

Self-awareness

The only constant in your life is yourself. You will always feel a sense of connection to the people you meet. In the end, self-esteem isn't just about 'me'. Self-esteem is about treating oneself as if you were a loved one, with the same regard, attention, and concern, care, and compassion that you would give to someone you care about.

In order to practise self-esteem, one must be aware of how they feel and what they need without being obsessive about it. I think it's about being aware of everything that has transpired in the past, present, and future and making wise decisions based on that information.

With self-esteem, you learn how to take care of yourself when things are going well and when they are not so well, so you may adopt and establish habits that will safeguard and sustain your well-being while also developing and improving it.

Taking care of yourself entails doing things differently if you're not already dealing with any of the problems listed below. Are you frequently confronted with which of the following?

Tiredness

- Sluggishness is making me feel sluggish.
- I'm in a state of disarray.
- Tension in the body..
- Inactivity and insufficient physical activity are the norm.
- Feeling angry and annoyed by the little things.
- Poor quality of sleep.
- Chronic or life-threatening sickness that recurs (colds, flu-like symptoms, infections).
- A lack of tranquilly.
- Having a bad day after being on social media for too long.

- Meal inconsistency.
- Eating a lot of junk food.
- Worry and anxiety.
- You can't turn off your thoughts.
- Depression at a moderate degree.
- Obligations and responsibilities are making you feel confined.
- There is not enough time to spend with loved ones..
- Too much time at the workplace, which is a problem.
- Irresponsibility in dealing with other people's needs and expectations
- Loneliness, emptiness, and isolation.
- Self-defeating and depressing ideas.
- Confidence and self-esteem are low.

Depression and mental health

When confronted with a situation that seems overwhelming or even devastating, knowing what's going on might be a lifesaver. Even though it's hard to believe, there's a solid explanation for your sorrow, astonishment, or despair. A good outcome may be found in all "bad" emotions, such as disappointment and shock. What's the constructive aim of this??Give yourself time to adjust to the new reality and accept that the old one is history. We have no choice but to accept it.

What if...? Is a common question you'll ask yourself when you reflect on past occurrences? "Why didn't I do this?" is a common question. in addition to the regretful phrase, "I regret doing this." When confronted with the reality of what has happened or is going to happen, it's common to have these types of thoughts.

If you're feeling down, don't be afraid to express it. "I shouldn't be so upset," you may think. Why am I so down?' Accepting melancholy for what it is - a transient and helpful feeling that may help you adapt to new and different situations – and learn to tolerate and live with them.

Disorientation and a lack of connection may set in. 'At times it seems like being somewhat intoxicated or concussed,' wrote C.S. Lewis following the loss of his wife. The world and I are separated by a thin veil. I have a hard time absorbing what others say.' Whether you've lost a loved one or endured a huge life shift now is the time to take care of yourself. Be kind with yourself and don't put too much pressure on yourself; your mind needs time to adjust to the new reality in your life. When you're sad, you're letting people know that you've lost or failed so that they may react in a way that's kind, compassionate, and supportive to you. So, treat yourself like a wonderful friend - with the same care and attention you would give to someone you care about. You should allow yourself to feel dejected from time to time.

People helping others on their own expense

Knowing what's going on may be a lifeline when presented with an overwhelming or even catastrophic scenario. Your grief, bewilderment or despair may be explained, even if you don't believe it. Disappointment and shock may also lead to positive outcomes. Exactly what is this supposed to accomplish?As you deal with the termination of your relationship, be gentle with yourself. There is nothing we can do but to accept it. "What if...?" is a common question when you reflect on the past. It's normal to wonder, "Why didn't I do this?" while also expressing regret, "I wish I hadn't done this," These ideas are quite typical while addressing a situation that has happened or is going to occur. Don't be scared to share your feelings if you're sad. You may think, "I shouldn't be so angry." Because I'm depressed. 'Acknowledging and appreciating sadness as a temporary and constructive mood that may aid you in adapting to new and different conditions. There may be feelings of disorientation and a lack of connection. After the death of his wife, C.S. Lewis wrote, "At times it looks like being slightly inebriated or concussed."Small distance separates me from the world. 'I have a hard time digesting what other people have to say. ' If you've just experienced the death of a loved one or a major change in your life, now is the time to prioritise your own well-being. In order for your mind to acclimate to the new reality in your life, be kind with yourself and don't stress yourself out. It is important to express your feelings of sadness to others so that they may respond in a manner that is kind, empathetic, and helpful to you when you are down. Take the same care and attention you would offer to a close friend while caring for yourself. Feeling down is normal, and should be encouraged.

Why they are late to recognize the red flags of their bad health

Everything you think, feel, and do has an impact on your life. Having a positive self-image leads to stronger relationships with friends and family..In order to make wise judgments and cope with life's difficulties, it is important to maintain a healthy mental state. Adolescents are prone to have difficulties with their mental health. In any given year, one out of every five teenagers in the United States has some kind of mental health issue.

Depending on their degree, the problems might range from minor to major. Suicide is the third leading cause of death among adolescents. " Most young people with mental health problems do not receive any treatment, which is tragic. Successful treatment approaches may assist a wide spectrum of ethnic and racial groups. You wouldn't wait to get medical attention if you fractured your limb or got pneumonia. Though they may be suffering from mental health concerns, many teenagers falsely feel that they will "snap out of it" or that they are a burden to society. Thus, people are left without the help they require in resolving their issues. You may have to adjust your expectations in order to get assistance. People with mental health issues go through significant physical and emotional suffering. An individual's prognosis is generally excellent if they get proper care. Inspiring success stories of young individuals with mental health issues are presented here. A person's sentiments of fear and anger will change throughout their lifetime.Understanding your personal mood swings and what triggers them is essential to your overall well-being.

There are several conditions that might induce emotional stress, such as a family breakup or strained friendships. For a while, you may feel depressed or "blue" after encountering difficult circumstances. That's not the same as suffering from a mental illness like depression. These feelings of helplessness and despair may last for months or even years for those who are suffering from depression. Suicidal thoughts and actions are possible outcomes of this depression. There are a number of symptoms that indicate the existence of a range of mental health issues or the need for assistance. Recognizing the following indications is critical:

- experiencing a sense of worthlessness or intense remorse
- sobbing uncontrollably for no apparent cause, retreating socially
- having an overwhelming sense of dread or terror
- extreme changes in mood or behaviour, such as binge eating or sleeping irregularly
- shaving a little amount of power
- a lack of enjoyment in previously enjoyed pastimes and activities
- having a hard time focusing or carrying out goals because of a surplus of energy
- a tendency to get quickly enraged or annoyed

Having thoughts that race or agitate you others not experiencing what you're hearing or seeing feeling that people are working against you in order to do damage to you or someone else. These indications aren't always simple to identify or understand. Accurate diagnoses can only be made by trained mental health specialists. According to a general rule of thumb, if the symptoms persist for a lengthy period of time, they are more likely to be severe and need medical attention.$$

Why people ignore mental breakdown

In today's fast-paced world, there are many emotional hurdles to overcome. All of these feelings might be triggered by the pressure to achieve and the urge to "keep up," as well as the desire for excellent connections and job fulfilment. As a result, we are taught in our culture to suppress and ignore our emotions. We're quite good at it: There are several methods to suppress our sensations, including drinking, using prescription drugs, and spending too much time in front of a computer. As soon as we notice them, we use mantras that we've memorized from infancy to fend them off. Mind over matter, get a grip, and buck up are just few of the more used phrases. Emotional suppression is detrimental to one's mental and physical well-being. Like hitting the gas and brakes at the same time in an automobile, it creates an internal pressure cooker that must be released quickly.

Our thoughts and body use a variety of innovative methods to tamp down our emotions, such as constricting our muscles and holding our breath. Many of today's common mental health issues, including anxiety and depression, can be traced back to the way we cope with our innate, hard-wired survival impulses. These are powerful biological forces that cannot be ignored. Psychiatric discomfort and symptoms may arise when the mind blocks the flow of emotions because they are overpowering or contradictory. Anxiety caused by unresolved emotions has been related to physical ailments including heart disease and intestinal illnesses as well as sleep disturbances and autoimmune diseases.

The majority of people are completely unaware of the power that their feelings have over them. However, if you recognise the power of emotions, even admitting your own may be really helpful. As an example, consider Frank, a patient of mine who was distraught because he couldn't afford the automobile he truly desired. When Frank's vehicle wish went unfulfilled, it set off a chain reaction of emotions including despair, rage, embarrassment, and worry. Even while Frank was aware that his stomach problems were related to stress, he was unaware that his excruciating stomach aches were being caused in part by his strong emotions. He had no idea how to feel better since he hadn't paid attention to his feelings.

Anxiety is said to increase when a person encounters more emotions and conflicts. In part, this is because of the vagus nerve, one of the body's primary emotional centres. It sends messages to the heart, lungs, and intestines in response to emotions aroused in the mid-brain. These signals prepare the body for quick and appropriate response in the interest of life. Emotions might be activated before the body has a chance to prepare for the response. It's the reason we can't consciously manage our emotions. When Frank spotted the automobile, he was overcome with feelings of grief, shame, and rage. His tummy began to churn almost immediately.

Even after Counselling, Frank's stomach pains persisted until he mastered the skill of tuning into his body to detect and name each emotion as it arose. Psychotherapy is increasingly emphasizing the role that emotions play in causing physical harm as well as recovering from it. Despite this, the field is still not considered part of the standard of care in the United States. In social work, doctorate programmes in psychology, and medical schools, emotional education is not required. Teaching folks that they can't control their emotions would be a huge benefit. Humans cannot regulate our emotions since they start in the part of our brain that is not under our control.

People, however, might begin to feel better if they are educated about their emotions and taught how to deal with them. Frank's stomach was healed when he allowed himself to be sad. It broke his heart that he couldn't acquire the automobile of his dreams. His anger was justified once he learned that it was normal. He also honed down on techniques for managing his rage in a manner that was beneficial to his well-being as well as the wellbeing of others around him. That diminished when he exercised self-compassion in response to his shame. His emotions faded when he had felt them all, as they always do when intensely sensed in the body. He was able to alleviate his stomach ache by altering the way his vagus nerve fired.

Contradictory sensations are often ignored by patients since that's what we've learned.That's why it's so important to feel the emotions that accompany our tales in order to repair our minds, because those emotions reside in our bodies. In order to feel and operate better, we must learn to recognise and engage with the basic emotions that are at the root of our worry.

Getting things done is probably not a problem for you if you simply push through life's unavoidable challenges. However, this tendency might make it easier to disregard your own psychological or emotional suffering at times. It requires a different type of strength to deal with your feelings, thoughts, and actions as honestly and objectively as possible. It's also not always clear when such skills should be put to use. For too long, you've been ignoring your mental health, and the consequences may be felt in many areas of your life.

Many people put off dealing with their mental health for a variety of reasons, according to clinical psychologist Deborah Offner, PhD. There's a popular belief that we must "tough it out," be "strong," or "independent," in order to succeed. There is a perception that seeking assistance is a sign of weakness or even self-indulgence. Despite the fact that mental health concerns are more widely recognised and accepted than ever before, the stigma associated with seeking help for them persists.

A lack of time or money might also be a barrier to seeking the care that is so much needed. Paying expenses, taking care of children and ageing relatives may all take precedence over attending to one's own mental health needs, as the saying goes.

If you don't take care of your mental health, it may affect everything from your relationships to your ability to sleep and perform at work. Everybody deserves mental health care, no matter what kind of aid you need, whether it's a support group or monthly get-togethers with friends.

According to Offner, irritation and impatience might be a sign that you're not dealing with anything that's upsetting you. Depression and anxiety may manifest as irritability, according to this expert. If you neglect your mental health for too long, you may get burnout.

Mental illness and sleep disorders are closely connected, according to the National Alliance on Mental Illness (NAMI). Sleep deprivation can increase the symptoms of mental illness, but the opposite is also true. If you're struggling to get a good night's sleep on your own, a doctor or therapist may be able to assist you in improving your mental health.

Mental health disorders like anxiety and sadness, on the other hand, might alter your eating habits over time. It's important to consider underlying mental health concerns if you observe a substantial change in your appetite that doesn't resolve immediately.

Dissatisfaction and apathy toward work might be indicators of burnout, according to doctors writing in the journal Pediatrics.Depression and anxiety may also have a negative impact on your ability to perform at work. Over time, being in a toxic job may have a negative impact on your emotional well-being. However, even if you like your work, problems with mental health may cause a variety of disruptions to your routine. If your job causes you a lot of stress, don't be afraid to get some help.

Self-care may need some alone time, but if you find yourself separating yourself from loved ones on a regular basis or your loneliness is becoming worse, you may have a mental health problem, according to Psychology Today..Get in touch with your loved ones to boost your overall health.

Chapter 5

Reclaim your dignity

Self-respect is something that many people overlook until it is completely destroyed. However, it might be tough to find the confidence to reconstruct what has been lost at this point.. While regaining one's self-respect isn't impossible, it does need a significant amount of work and willpower.

However, how can you learn to respect yourself if you don't really value yourself at the moment? Here are some methods for regaining or regaining your self-respect, as well as maintaining it. Be confident in your ability to rebuild. Knowing that you can regain your self-respect after you've lost it is critical for your general well-being. It's only real if you believe it is.If you don't, you'll always be unhappy with yourself. To succeed in this rebuilding process, you must retain a positive outlook on your efforts and work hard at it. It's human nature to make errors. Your self-esteem will suffer if you keep blaming yourself for your mistakes. Accept your mistakes, promise to improve, then follow through.

Focus on what is important to you rather than what other people think. As you work to improve your life, you are likely to face criticism. Self-pity, poor self-esteem, and an absence of self-respect may be preferred by certain individuals. A strange occurrence is that some people choose to surround themselves with others who are in a bad situation because it makes them feel better about themselves. Remain true to your essential views and ideals instead than caring about what other people think. Self-respect will return to your life as a result of this.

For those who care about what others think, the answer is to adjust your self-perception and how you see others. Instead of worrying that others are trying to get you or that everyone else seems to have it all together but you, develop the more proactive belief that most people have your best interests at heart and want you well. Encourage your own attempts to develop and restore your self-respect by giving yourself a pep talk. As a matter of fact, this is an essential aspect of general health and living a meaningful life. Make ambitious plans for your future and work hard to realise them.

You can restore the harm done to your self-esteem by keeping yourself to high standards, even if you've done terrible things in the past. Now is a good moment to adopt high standards, if you lacked them in the past.Give it your all and don't settle for anything less than that.. Pride yourself on keeping your end of the bargain and doing what you say you'll do.Honesty, hard work, and devotion are three of life's most vital virtues.. You may begin to gain self-respect if you begin with these steps.

The notion that you can create or re-establish your self-respect and hold yourself to higher standards, as well as the effort you've previously put in, are both essential. You're more likely to stick with your goals if you have a strategy in place.. To help you keep track of your progress, you can also look back and see how far you've come, as well as how far you still have to go.

You will find it simpler to do the right thing if you keep a persistent objective of living in truth and in accordance with your values and beliefs. As a result, you won't feel as compelled as before to do things that are inconsistent with what you believe in or what's important to you. Follow your inner advice and take action.. Rebuilding one's self-esteem might take as long as the process of losing one's self-respect. Self-respect is a topic that many people have never given much consideration to, but now is a great opportunity to consider the benefits of treating yourself with the utmost respect and admiration. Things that are most essential to you will come first... A lot of us have a tendency of reliving something that someone said to us in our brains over and over again. As an alternative to blaming ourselves and blaming others, Jackson advocates extending empathy and understanding to all parties.

Make a habit of writing down the instances in which you make a good difference in the lives of others. Finally, they aren't limited to grand gestures. Somebody with a lot of luggage may have appreciated it if you held the door open for them. Alternatively, you may have begun making a new pot of coffee at work when you discovered that the previous one had run out of beans For those who have trouble shifting their mindset, Jackson suggests thinking of it this way: "Tomorrow is a new day, so let you off the hook and start fresh tomorrow."

Weight Gain and Minimal social interaction

Socioeconomic factors are also affected by several sorts of health-related societal difficulties. For example, the CDC estimates that 18.5% of American People are overweight or obese, with a BMI of 95 percent or more. However, not all children are equally affected by the pandemic of childhood obesity. There is a significant reduction in childhood obesity among people whose parents have better levels of education and earnings, as compared to children from poorer socioeconomic backgrounds.

Bullying may also be affected by obesity, which is a major societal problem. Many students are harassed because of their weight or other outward appearance difficulties, according to the PACER National Bullying Prevention Center. Despite recent anti-bullying efforts, more than 20% of American people say they have been bullied at some point in their school careers. One-third of the people who have been bullied indicate that it occurs at least once or twice every month. More over a quarter (28 percent) of middle school kids say they have been bullied online.

Every part of our well-being depends on our ability to engage with others. Emotional and physical well-being may be improved by having a strong support system or strong community ties, according to research.Numerous studies have shown the relevance of social support in improving one's physical and mental well-being over the course of time.

an individual's attempt to manage the impact they have on others via social interactions. They want a positive response. There is a desire to seem trustworthy. Meanwhile, the others want to make sure the individual is sincere, trustworthy, and all-around likeable before they spend any time with. Meeting someone in person in "real time" may not provide them access to the individual's past. For this reason, they contrast what a person says about themselves with the unintended "give-offs," such as their facial expressions, mannerisms, gestures, anxiety, the quality of their attire, the application of their make-up, and the language they use. There are a variety of micro-level mechanisms that control social interactions regardless of their unique content because of this dynamic.

An important part of social interaction is the exchange of power that takes place when people get together in groups. Meetings in which participants are physically present for a certain period of time are often referred to as "face-to-face" meetings. Social contacts that are technology mediated like texting, skyping or messaging may also be thought of in modern society When it comes to sociology's four levels of analysis—micro, meso,Social interactions are explored at the micro and macro levels, where the pre-established patterns of behaviour that people are expected to follow in various social contexts are examined in detail.situations, can be examined. Gender inequality and historical transitions have a direct influence on the micro-level processes of daily life, according to the sociology of emotions. The ability to regulate one's impressions effectively needs an awareness of both one's own expressions and those of one's surroundings. Using this method, the cynical side of social interaction's impression management is explored.

Building Confinedence

A lot of us get bogged down in our thoughts and some of us more than others. Many of our ideas are not very positive, even if it is nice to examine life and wonder about oneself. It's easy to become caught up in the minutiae of life, such as wondering why your spouse was a douchebag the other night or why a colleague claimed credit for your work today, while we're in mind-wandering mode (also known as "in your head"). Interestingly, the brain's default mode network (DMN) is "on" while we're not paying attention to anything in particular during these moments, meaning that our thinking is often predicated on concern.

When your thoughts stray from what you're doing, it's far more difficult to remain content. Harvard researchers a few years back utilised a specially created iPhone app to ask participants what they were doing at odd times of the day, whether they were thinking about that work, and how happy/unhappy they felt. The article's title, "A wandering mind is a dissatisfied mind," echoed the conclusion. As a result, the objective is to return to the here and now. For millennia, psychologists and philosophers have debated how to do this. A few tried-and-true (and science-based) techniques to help you re-engage with the current moment are provided below.

To that end, making new friends – even if you don't know them – is an excellent way to get out of your shyness, especially in the age of the iPhone. In a recent study at the University of Chicago, researchers showed that when volunteers were encouraged to engage in conversation with a complete stranger on a train or bus, their moods improved significantly, as well as the stranger's mood. Because we desire to connect with one another, even if we don't know whether anybody else wants to, this may be the case. They do in fact. So go a bit over the line, but not so much as to frighten off the other person, but enough to show them that you're open for a little more intimacy. The other option is to engage in small-talk with your seatmate on the bus. Not to mention that it will brighten both your and his days.

Giving to your self

While flying, an oxygen mask will be placed in front of you. What's your occupation? Putting on one's own oxygen mask comes first, as we've all learned. We can only successfully assist others if we first help ourselves. As a caregiver, one of the most critical—and sometimes overlooked—tasks is taking care of one's own needs. The individual you are caring for will benefit as well when your needs are met.

To be clear, self-care does not imply selfishness. In reality, the exact reverse is true. One of the many advantages of practicing self-care is that it strengthens your immune system and gives you more energy.Things go awry and you're better prepared to bounce back when they don't. In other words, taking care of oneself improves your ability to care for other people. At work or in any other scenario, you may also provide your utmost effort. As a result, taking care of one's self is not optional. It's a vital part of a happy, healthy, and successful existence.

As a result, having objectives might be useful since they guide you in the right path. Stopping smoking, lowering stress, curing a physical condition like diabetes, or regaining your mental health are all examples of self-care.

It doesn't matter what you're trying to do, establish what success looks like, and set a reasonable deadline for achieving those objectives. It's a good idea to create milestone objectives as you move along. The first milestone may be a week without smoking, then a month, then a month without smoking, and so on. As you work toward your long-term objective, you'll find it simpler to remain motivated this way. Self-awareness is a very potent therapeutic tool. Regular self-monitoring may help you discover detrimental thinking patterns or recognise when you're on the verge of descending into self-destructive behaviour."

Write for three pages in your journal every morning as soon as you wake up, about whatever that comes to mind. To identify and overcome obstacles, review these notes on a regular basis. Having a supportive community around you might also help you keep on track with your self-care goals. As a result, you feel a feeling of belonging to something higher than yourself, which may help you understand your own importance and spark pleasure in your life.

When it comes to self-care, there's no right or wrong, but it's easy to get caught up in the "shoulds." In this way, self-care is reduced to a chore to be crossed off a list. If you don't like the idea of waking up at 5 a.m. to meditate, find something else that works for you. Your self-care routines will be more successful and enjoyable if you follow your passions.

Consider how you can better take care of your body.

Eat for overall health and well-being

Did you know that your mental and emotional well-being and physical health are intertwined?

Reduce your intake of refined sweets, caffeine, alcohol, and highly processed meals by including more fruits and vegetables into your diet. Intuitive eating is something else you may want to have a look at learning.

Ensure that you consume a lot of fluids.

When you're dehydrated, your immune system, heart health, and metabolic rate all suffer, and your mood and ability to concentrate are all negatively affected. In order to stay hydrated, adults should drink around two-thirds of their body weight in ounces of water per day. Drink 130 ounces of water per day if you weigh 200 pounds.

Make sure you get a fair amount of sleep.

The number of hours of sleep required by each individual is unique. Between seven and nine hours of sleep is required by adults each night.

If you have trouble falling asleep at night because of insomnia, consider establishing a bedtime ritual that will aid in your relaxation. Relaxation strategies, lowering coffee consumption, and avoiding screens two hours before bedtime are just a few ideas.

Moving your body

Getting your blood pumping is essential for a healthy body and mind. In addition to boosting your energy levels, exercising helps alleviate stress and sleeplessness, as well as improving your general health. Climbing a mountain or taking samba lessons are both great ways to get your heart pumping.

Get a firm grip on reality.

Walking barefoot, sitting, or resting on the ground is known as "grounding." The immune system is calmed, inflammation is reduced, pain is relieved, and general health is promoted by this simple act. Finding a place where you can remove your shoes and go barefoot on the ground is all it takes. At least 20 minutes should be spent doing this.

While perfection is no longer required, there is always room for improvement. Self-esteem may be boosted through doing activities that you love, as well as recognising and recognising your strengths. All of us tend to excel at the things we're most passionate about, and we tend to love doing the things we're best at. We love doing the things we're excellent at, and we're more likely to enjoy doing those things if we're passionate about them.What are some of your favourite pastimes? The choice is yours. Is it possible that you have a voice? Fishing? Do you play an instrument? Running? Are you going to be taking part in any football activities? Attending historical reenactments?

Taking Mental Care

Meditation may help alleviate stress and anxiety, as well as improve emotional and mental well-being. Practicing meditation on a regular basis may also assist to enhance blood flow and sleep, as well as lessen dependency on drugs and alcohol.

It's essential to build a grateful mindset.

Gratitude writing might help you feel more relaxed. As a result, it aids the immune system, builds emotional fortitude, and promotes sound sleep. It may also help you build better connections with other people.

Set reasonable limits for yourself.

The benefits of setting limits include increased energy levels, lessened stress, and a reduced risk of burnout. Being able to express your wants to others in a way that they can understand can help to keep your relationships healthy and free of conflict. It is possible to boost mood and indirectly care for yourself by spending time with people if you are able to control your limits.

Spend time outside in the fresh air.

Spending at least two hours each week in nature has been shown to improve both mental and physical health. Do your best to take use of the nearby green areas and parks, even if you live in the city.

Tenth, take charge of your stress.

Managing stress may be done in many different ways... Listed below are a few suggestions you may wish to give a shot:

- Breathing exercises
- Reading a great book
- Taking part in a yoga session
- a stroll in the park
- Taking use of the available light
- The act of playing with a pet

Studies show that giving back, or prosociality, has both immediate and long-term health benefits for the physical, mental, and emotional well-being of people. Donate your time, money, or abilities in some manner. There is nothing wrong with writing your thoughts and emotions down in a journal as an alternative to talking to someone. Students who journaled about their emotions on a daily basis went to the doctor less often, according to one research.

Hire an expert to assist you.

You can become unstuck by getting an outsider's perspective on what's holding you back, like a counsellor or coach. With virtual sessions, it's possible to discover a match no matter where in the globe you are.

Empowering yourself with knowledge

Knowledge is a state or reality of being acquainted with something because of one's own experiences or because of one's connections to it. It's a process in which you gather a wide variety of data and come to a thorough grasp of the subject at hand. A person's capacity to differentiate right from wrong is enhanced when they have access to knowledge. An important part of embracing knowledge is the process of educating yourself so that you can make well-informed choices and have a clear sense of what is best for your future.

It's possible to learn new things, but you have to be prepared to expand yourself and be open to new experiences. It's up to every one of us to take advantage of the possibilities that God offers us. You have to take advantage of the opportunities that are there in front of you if you want to succeed in your job. Are you open to making adjustments in order to advance in your professional life? The single most essential thing you can do to advance your professional career is to immerse yourself in as much knowledge as possible. If you don't want to learn and grow, you'll have a hard time succeeding in your work. In other words, if you're not eager to learn new things and expand your horizons, you won't be able to advance in your profession. Only you are capable of making this choice.

Changing your life and the world begins with learning new things. Knowledge is more than just a source of power; it is the foundation of empowerment. The more you learn, the more equipped you are to take charge of your life in a variety of ways. This is why so many of our so-called "leaders" go to great lengths to undermine the authority of the people around them. People who are self-assured need less advice and direction from others who aren't themselves empowered. When you're empowered, you're in charge of your own destiny.

It's easy to start a fight by spreading misinformation and fabricating laws that violate basic human rights. As a result of conflict, the collective consciousness tends to look outside for solutions rather than inside. When we rely on other people to tell us what to do or how to solve our problems, we are robbing ourselves of our own agency. This is not the same as going through the motions of studying and picking up knowledge as you go. Perspective and insight may be gained by reading books and blogs, as well as from studying the sciences and the humanities. The point is not to give up your power, but rather to pull more of it into yourself.

As opposed to turning to someone else for guidance, this is a process of discovering your own path. What's the deal here? Mindfulness is the obvious solution to this question. Your ideas and emotions have greater power over you when you become more conscious of them. Ultimately, this provides you an edge.

What are the areas in which you have sway?

It's difficult to exercise any influence on the outer world. Nobody else can make decisions for you since you have no control over them. All you have control over is your thoughts and feelings, not your hair or clothing style. To achieve this, one must engage in regular meditation and other forms of awareness training.

To practise mindfulness, you must become aware of your thoughts and feelings. You have complete control over what you think and how you feel about the world around you. It's true that this will be influenced by external factors such as events, people and situations. As a result of physical and mental abuse, you will think and feel in specific ways that are unique to the situation at hand.

The choice is yours once the first shock has worn off. How strongly do you hold to the feelings and concepts you gained from the experience? As a matter of fact, are they a part of your daily life? There's no right or wrong answer. If it's something good, you'll probably want to put some effort into boosting its energy and increasing its scope. However, if this is something undesirable, you'll likely want to concentrate on reducing or eliminating it. However, the unpleasant thoughts and emotions that arise from external events and influences tend to persist at times. Because we aren't always aware of how they affect us, we tend to cling on to them.

Let's get back to the subject of frequency by taking a look at the following.Positive energy is associated with high frequencies, whereas negative energy is associated with low frequencies. However, in today's culture, the shortage, scarcity, and fear-base is part of the issue. Negativity is hard to avoid when everyone's thinking about it all the time, since like attracts like. After being influenced, mindfulness may help you decide what to do next. This is a tremendous amount of information. The concepts of book smarts and street smarts, as well as the contrasts between the two, are often discussed. Emotional-smarts, on the other hand, are the focus here. For as long as I can remember, as a D&D fan, I've seen this as being related to character creation. Each character's statistics, which have an effect on the various classes of characters and their skills, are determined by rolling dice for each of the characters. Two of these attributes are wit and intelligence. On the practical level, I view the difference between intelligence and wisdom as a difference between those who are book clever and those who are street smart. So, what role does emotional intelligence plays in this scenario? Emotional-smarts, in the real world, is what connects these two concepts. You learn how to be a book smart student in school. Street etiquette is best learned by hands-on experience. Book smarts and street smarts both have the potential to arouse emotions in people. It's for this reason that emotional intelligence is so important.triumphs over rational intelligence.Being attentive is being observant of your thoughts and feelings. It's not simply a fleeting thought of them, but a full knowledge of what you're thinking and feeling. Being aware of what's going on within your thoughts gives you the ability to better hold onto or let go of certain emotions. This is a really liberating development.

Negativity and hype about what we CAN'T accomplish are all too easy to believe in. Lacking and fear-based culture tries to persuade you there is no way. As a result of cultivating mindfulness, you will be able to better influence and manage your own thoughts and feelings.TEmpowerment comes from wearing a hat. As a result, it might have a significant effect on the situation.Your ideas and feelings are entirely under your control. That is the epitome of discernment. As a result, you gain a sense of empowerment and self-determination. In the end, it is critical that you acknowledge that you are deserving and worthy of this power. This is not widely accepted. There is a lot of pressure from the outside world to achieve a certain degree of accomplishment in order to be considered successful. What counts is that you are deserving of your life and are making the most of it. To put it another way, knowledge is a kind of power that can be used to empower oneself. Empowerment allows you to see yourself in a new light. All throughout your life, you are able to learn, develop, and change. It is only when you place yourself in an awkward situation that you become trapped. You can always discover a solution that works for you, no matter how daunting the process may appear. You don't need to do anything remarkable to earn them if you want them. Nobody is here merely to get by; you were put here to do more than just exist. Be as knowledgeable as you can, be aware of your ideas and emotions, and see what you can do to develop the life you most want.

Chapter 6

Fend for Yourself

People are seeking an excuse to "Treat Yourself" may not be doing it enough. Neither is a two-month comprehensive yoga retreat essential. Put on some music and shake the bottle your mother gave you for a few minutes to acquire some nutrition. We may all feel exhausted, agitated, and overwhelmed if we don't make time for ourselves. Here comes self-care, the one who holds you close and assures you that everything will be OK. It was impossible to improve one's self after the seventh day in pajama bottoms, even during a worldwide pandemic when many of us had more free time than we knew what to do with. Working till your eyes bleed or spending months in lockdown with nothing to do appears to be the norm in the 21st century. But even now, even more than before, it's essential to practice self-compassion and priorities self-care. It's been said a million times, but the lesson remains the same: go slow and steady to win the race. To have a positive impact on your life, whether it's getting more exercise, cleaning up your house, or improving your interpersonal connections, you need to put in the time. Begin by answering the following questions: You may start small, of course!

One tiny modification in your daily routine can have you feeling better, happier, and more prepared for everything life throws your way. In the event that your grand goals (such as reducing sugar intake or organizing your whole wardrobe) fail to take hold, consider the following: Is your workload too much for you to handle? The Good Housekeeping Institute's health experts and product aficionados believe that small, realistic objectives may have a huge effect. Self-care suggestions gained on the job are being shared here, including minor lifestyle modifications that might help you feel less stressed and more satisfied and more motivated to take on your objectives in 2022."

So, What?

Self-care is any activity or habit that assists a person in avoiding health concerns, which is often overlooked yet very required. Excessive stress, for example, may raise your chance of developing heart disease. As a result, stress alleviation has the potential to assist someone in keeping their ticker ticking.

Maintaining and improving our mental and physical health via self-care may be beneficial since it may increase our sense of self-worth, stress management skills, and overall well-being.These activities contribute to the maintenance of equilibrium in a world that is becoming progressively overstimulating. Taking care of oneself is a crucial component of living a lifestyle that keeps us healthy, joyful, and more in touch with our minds and bodies. The trouble is that you are most likely not doing nearly enough of it. You may easily blend self-care and indulgence when it comes to your food and drink choices.. This perspective may cause us to feel guilty for believing that we need to spend time away from our hectic schedule doing something that, simply expressed, helps us feel better about ourselves. Not only is it vital to be fair to yourself and let good, nutritious things into your life, but it is also critical that you understand where your own boundary is.Self-indulgence is made up of quick solutions that only last a short time.

Even if you're not a big fan of sweets, they may be enjoyed in moderation.However, short bursts of indulgence are not a permanent path to health and pleasure — and they may also have negative consequences for others. Students' nurses may overlook their own health and wellness requirements while learning to care for others, according to 2019 research. This, in turn, may impair their efficacy while giving care to the general public. As a result, it's not a bad idea to periodically check in with your body and mind. Checking in with oneself may be beneficial, so it's worth the effort. Rather than being self-serving, the quest for health and pleasure is a noble endeavor. If we maintain proper care of ourselves, we are more likely to see improvements in a variety of facets of our life, including our physical health and our interpersonal interactions. In turn, this puts us in a better position to help the individuals we care about most in the world.

A plan of Action

Due to the fact that self-care is a very personalized activity, there is no specific formula for how or when to go about doing it.Make it a point to do something that brings you joy at least once a day. Have you reached the end of your creative wits? Do not be alarmed.Listed here are some delicious ways for reducing stress, increasing happiness, and enhancing general health. Practice any of these self-care habits (or any others that come to mind) on a daily, monthly, or even hourly basis, depending on how it feels most comfortable for you.

Get out into the fresh air.

Try a workout in the outdoor air

Giving up your familiar surroundings is an excellent method to enhance both your mental and physical well-being.Exercising your body and mind outside provides similar benefits to those of meditation.Observation of nature photographs has been shown to elicit a pleasant response in the brain, according to other studies. So, if you're unable to go out into nature right away, check out your Mac's default screensaver. Perhaps out the window would suffice. Although if you reside in a place with lots of greenery (fields and lawns), you'll be healthier and less worried. Also, make an effort to spend time in the garden; it's a fantastic place to get some exercise without being seen. Consider taking your workout outside as well. According to research, exercising outside is more beneficial to those who are depressed than exercising in a gym. Another research indicated that persons who engage in outdoor physical activity feel more refreshed and energized, as well as less stressed, confused, melancholy, and irritable.

It's time to pay something forward

If someone wants to be prominent and nice at the same time, you need both. We gain from assisting others, but we also learn from it ourselves. Lending a helping hand may improve one's mental health as well as one's lifespan. Is generosity genuinely altruistic if you also benefit?In my opinion, you're making people happy. Your taste buds will be delighted by the experience as a consequence.Self-esteem, confidence, and general well-being can all benefit from volunteering. A simple grin can be infectious, so it's no wonder that helping others makes you feel good. Gratitude expert Emily Fletcher, creator of Ziva Meditation, thinks humans thrive when they are helpful. "Volunteering helps individuals to feel more present since the reward is in the act itself." Studies have shown that volunteering, particularly if it becomes a habit, has long-term advantages, which you may have heard about before.

Take in the appropriate fragrances

Breathing exercises have been shown to help us relax. It's not simply how we breathe that's crucial, though. When life hands your lemons, citrus fragrances — especially orange essential oil — may help reduce stress and anxiety. At the same time, experts continue to debate the advantages of aromatherapy. For some individuals, a breath of rosemary might improve their memory. The scent is, of course, immensely individual; what one person finds relaxing, another finds irritating. It's possible, though, to create an atmosphere that matches your schnozzle and calms you down by stocking up on your favorite smells.

Conscious and deliberate breathing exercises have been shown to reduce blood pressure, increase emotions of peace and serenity, and alleviate stress. It is hard to say how effective breathing exercises are in the long run, but many experts believe they may help you develop more self-awareness and a more Zen outlook.

Assuage your anxiety

Ugh. Stress. We've all experienced it, and if you haven't, you've probably never gone to a family lunch. The effects on your health may be detrimental if you're always stressed out.

When it comes to self-care, this is where it comes in.

As a society, we've come to accept that stress has a detrimental effect on our health. Stress can have a harmful impact on cardiovascular health. It's impossible to avoid feeling overwhelmed by life's demands, though, whether it's a job, in personal relationships, with family, or in any other capacity. Don't let yourself be swayed. Drinking tea and practicing progressive relaxation may help you keep the stress monster away.

Relaxation techniques for stress relief

- You should contract and then relax every muscle group in your body as you go from your fingertips to your toes. Relaxing the body and mind go hand in hand. In studies, this method has been shown to reduce anxiety and sadness.

- Yoga is a powerful stress reliever because of its blend of deep breathing methods and yoga positions. It was shown to be effective among college students, a demographic that tends to be prone to stress. Distinct types of yoga exist, from gentle to vigorous. Because of its soft motions, hatha yoga may be particularly effective in helping you relax.

- Are you not a fan of meditation? Just concentrate on breathing. Stress and anxiety may be reduced by taking a few deep breaths from the diaphragm, according to research.

Be cautious of your surroundings

Focusing on the here and now, without evaluating our feelings or thoughts, maybe both freeing and healthful. Mindfulness is a term for this practice, and it has grown more popular in psychiatric treatment. Research has also shown that mindfulness training, then being more in touch with our inner selves, helps us feel better and reduces stress. It may also prevent your thoughts from wandering, which is a benefit.

Take pleasure in yourself

We're sure of it. It's much simpler to say than to do, isn't it? It's nice to be happy. I mean, come on. But it's also good for your health, which is a bonus. Health and happiness go hand-in-hand. Having a positive outlook on life may even help avoid heart disease, according to new research. "Be cheerful" might be a challenge for some people, but it turns out there's an easy approach to boost your mood: Just grin!

Meditate

One of the benefits of meditation is that it doesn't need a lot of time to be beneficial to the mind and body. It doesn't matter if you simply have a few minutes to yourself; emptying your mind can help alleviate stress.Compassion and emotional stability are also improved as a result of meditation. According to some studies, meditation may even help people avoid contracting winter diseases by improving their quality of life. Isn't it the best? Even when we're not meditating, the advantages are still there - consider it a present to yourself. Any excuse you use to not meditate should be met with a corresponding amount of practice time. Mindfulness practices may be used as a shorthand meaning "I have no time to spend in my well-being."

Make a merry jig

Baby Shark is a last resort. Other than that, they're not that significant. A variety of dances are acceptable. In addition to burning calories, shaking your body is a great way to tone up. It may also lead to a higher quality of life, a decreased risk of dementia, and new and interesting social contacts and friendships.

Increase the volume of the music

The fact that some tunes make you grin isn't a unique phenomenon. Research, it seems out, has accepted the fact as well. Exposure to happy songs has been shown to assist in encouraging creative thinking, according to research.Playing music is also beneficial to one's health.

Eat more fruits and veggies to be healthy.

When we consume more fresh produce, we are practicing ego during the day. Fruits have been seen in research to enhance mental performance. Parkinson's would be much less probable if you consume peppers often. And if we needed another incentive to eat more fruits and vegetables, consuming seven servings a day might make us happy. We'd run out of room if we attempted to list all of the health benefits of every vegetable. Cooking them this way will ensure that they retain their nutritional value. Neat.

Make a pact with yourself

Most places (work, church, a date, meeting your date's parents, during your wedding speech... you get the idea) are inappropriate for a potty mouth. However, an F-bomb might be a quick and simple method to vent some frustration. Swearing has been shown to relieve physical discomfort and even to increase one's self-esteem and confidence, according to research. But, as the saying goes, timing is key, so be careful not to disgrace yourself more by letting loose with your expletives.

Allow yourself to indulge in some shopping therapy

Shopaholics, rejoice: Purchasing new clothing, according to research conducted in 2011, may improve your attitude. To put joy on your face before resorting to scientific research, all you need is to buy yourself something sparkly, unique, and new (it doesn't have to cost a fortune). You should avoid making poor financial decisions, but at the same time, you should avoid depriving yourself of pleasures due to a false feeling of guilt. Taking this step if you're short on money will only make things worse.A goal or savings plan for something you truly desire may work, though!

Put your best foot forward

Obviously, not everyone has this choice. Even if you don't like the way sex makes you feel, there are a plethora of benefits to having sex. To improve our immune system's ability to defend us, we need to stay active. Just a few of its health advantages include reducing stress and alleviating migraine discomfort. It may even reduce the stress-induced rise in blood pressure. Just remember that your Spotify Sexy Music playlist is exactly what the doctor prescribed the next time you put it on.

Become a voracious reader

Despite what some middle school bullies assume, reading is cool. In addition, reading is beneficial to our health in other ways. Trying to read on a regular basis was shown to keep the mind sharp as it ages, according to studies. As a result of reading fiction, you will be more creative and have a more open mind. Opening a book may also help us sleep better and increase our capacity for empathy, all of which are beneficial if you want to be a well-rounded, upstanding individual.Make the most of your time away from home by reading a good book.

Despite my best efforts, I couldn't hold back my laughter.

Why? Because of the aforementioned LOL. Laughter really is the best medicine, as the saying goes. Mental and physical well-being may be improved by laughing, particularly when paired with physical activity. It's important for our wellness and very well to have a good chuckle from time to time, and it's also good for our relationships with those we laugh with. Your strategy: Make time for some lighthearted entertainment, such as repeats of "How I Met Your Mother" (until the last season, which is just bad for your life).

Take a look at something adorable

Looking at photographs of cute infant animals is a quick way to lift your spirits. We don't know how to assist you if you don't feel better after gazing at puppies, kittens, and newborn dolphins. That's a cinch now, thanks to Pinterest (check out this board, which is jam-packed with adorable animal buddies). In addition, looking through these images may even assist you in your professional life. According to several studies, it may help you be more productive at work. It's also possible to bring your employer along if you're lucky enough to work at Greatest.

Make sure you get adequate sleep

Things like staying up late at work, having a wild night out with friends, or even simply watching "Scandal" might keep us from getting enough shut-eye. One of the dangers of not getting enough sleep is that it decreases our ability at work, increases our appetite, and increases our risk of developing health problems, including heart disease and type 2 diabetics. Even if it's only a little catnap over your lunch break, make sleep a priority for a healthier, happier you.

Enjoy the benefits of a massage.

Relax and unwind with a massage at a time that works for you.. It is calming to the mind and body, and it helps you have a better night's sleep by lowering your stress levels. We delved into the science of massages and what they can do for you. When a masseuse manipulates the body's muscles and soft tissues to alleviate pain or reduce tension, it's considered massage therapy. However, not all massages are the same! Strategies include deep tissue massage (often referred to as Swedish massage) and reflexology, in which the therapist puts pressure on a particular area of the body to ease the pain. In addition, massage may be utilized to address a wide range of health issues. Massage treatment has been shown to alleviate pain, induce muscular relaxation, and enhance mood and sleep quality in recent research. Another research indicated that respondents' salivary cortisol levels dropped after being massaged, a stress-inducing hormone. According to one research, massage therapy's enjoyable aspects might contribute to enhanced body image among its beneficiaries, particularly in women.

Surrounding yourself with Positivity

In business, economics, and relationships, we all want success. So, why is it that so few individuals are happy in all of these different ways?

The solution lies inside your own expectations. To alter your life, your career, and your relationship, Tony advises, you must elevate your standards. Get rid of those that are a drain on your energy. When you surround yourself with people who encourage you, share their wisdom and help you grow from your errors, you will be more successful. Set a high standard for yourself and those who are closest to you. You may trace this idea back to at least 6th century BC Confucius, who published one of the first lines about surrounding oneself with excellent people: "If you're the wisest person in a room, then you've got a problem." You can utilize the principle of becoming who you surround yourself with to accomplish your goals in business and in life because it's real.

Is it effective to think positively? Maintaining sobriety or escaping domestic abuse can only be achieved if you surround yourself with positive-thinking people. In the end, a great deal of optimistic thinking is influenced by the individuals you associate with. There's no need to limit yourself to solely spending time with those who are "perfect," though.Those that motivate and encourage you to strive for greater heights should be surrounded by like-minded others. They're encouraging you to stay clean and sober by offering you their help and encouragement. When you open up to them about your experiences with domestic violence, they'll be there to support you emotionally. Negative people, on the other hand, are more likely to have a negative influence on your life. However, it doesn't matter if these folks are related to you or are just workers of your company. They really care about your well-being and want to see you succeed.

In order to remain focused on your long-term objectives, surround yourself with people that inspire you. You'll have a better self-image. Spending time with these individuals will leave you feeling energized and driven. Your stress levels will drop. When you're surrounded by like-minded people, it's much easier to stay on course. As a result, your self-esteem will soar. When you spend time with these folks, you'll be stimulated and inspired. Your stress levels will go down.

Importance of Positivity

"You are who you hang out with," someone once said to you. If you're a parent, you're probably concerned about your children hanging out with the wrong crowd. Your parents probably were, too. Why? Because your emotions, views of the world, and expectations of yourself are influenced by the people you spend the most time with. We intuitively know this as parents, and we want to make the most of the influence we have on our children via the power of proximity. So, why don't we put it to good use?

In any element of your life, having excellent friends and associates may have a positive impact. Similar to how you gain when you surround yourself with individuals who make you happy, those in your professional or social circles who are pessimistic or narrow-minded may harm you.

Putting Money Into Your Own Pocket

Making investments in oneself is one of the smartest investments you can make! Putting Money Into Your Own

Pocket, on the other hand, is generally a low-priority item, something we'd want to accomplish eventually.

Our excuses for delaying life-enriching activities include a lack of time and money. The fact that you may not have a lot of free time or money to invest in yourself is true, but it's also crucial to note that we frequently claim these reasons because we fail to perceive the genuine worth of investing in ourselves.

Either we don't believe in ourselves enough to take the risk, or we've convinced ourselves that the benefits will be insufficient to justify the investment. Unless we take the risk and attempt new things, we'll never be able to improve ourselves. We're worth it.

We're overworking ourselves, and that's the only solution. The mere act of attempting something new may nonetheless have a major impact on your life. There are several advantages to starting something different, whether it's going to a new location, learning a new skill, or enrolling in a class. All of these factors may aid in our personal growth and development, allowing us to reach our full potential.

Investing in your own well-being has several advantages.

Just a few examples:

- An enormous feeling of success and contentment is yours when you make an effort to care for yourself. There is nothing like the feeling of success that comes from accomplishing or completing anything that might have a good impact on your mental health and well-being.

- Our deepest apprehension about making self-investments stems from a sense of unworthiness or the fear that we won't be able to get the full rewards of our efforts. When you commit to anything, whether it's signing up for a class, going to the doctors, or trekking a mountain, you'll feel more confident and optimistic. Possessing self-assurance opens the door to achieving more than you ever imagined possible, as well as raising the bar on your ambitions and overcoming any doubts you may have had about your ability to succeed in the past.

- New relationships may be formed as a result of putting money into your own development. Investing in people and relationships that matter a lot to you may help both you and the people you care about to become stronger. Having a good buddy can go a long way! If you're parleying whether or not to chase a new endeavor or opportunity that will enhance your life, don't put it off until "someday." There will never be a point in our lives when we aren't busy or don't have money to spend. You should instead ask yourself whether or not it's something you'd want to do. That depends on whether or not the response is "yes." Don't allow anything to stop you from achieving your dreams. The investment you make in yourself, whatever it is, will produce both immediate and long-term benefits. Your life will become more stable when you take the time to engage in something that will benefit you mentally—whether it's acquiring new talent or honing an existing one. Many of us sacrifice our own abilities in order to put our employer's needs ahead of our own. However, keep in mind that no job is ever completely safe from losing.

Chapter 7

Reclaiming Self-Esteem and Self-Respect

It's all too easy to overlook the significance of having positive self-esteem. However, having positive self-respect may be the difference between feeling good about yourself and taking care of your needs and not feeling good about yourself and not taking care of your needs.

We've all heard the advice to believe in yourself, respect yourself, be your own cheerleader, and that you can't completely love people until you love yourself—and all of that is true. But what about believing in yourself? But, in practice, what does this entails in terms of meaning is unclear. Self-esteem is an essential component of a successful and happy life.

But how can you know whether your self-esteem is high enough? What are the signs? Throughout this section, we'll discuss what self-esteem is, why it's essential, and how to increase your own.

On the topic of self-esteem, we'll discuss the negative consequences of low self-esteem, the difference between being down on yourself a few times a year and having truly low self-esteem, the factors that contribute to low self-esteem, and strategies for cultivating a more positive image of oneself and self-respect.

A person's self-esteem may be either high or low, depending on how they feel about themselves. When we think that we are good and worthwhile and that others see us in a favorable light, we feel good about ourselves. When we think that we are less than others, we experience low self-esteem as a negative emotion.

Many things influence our sense of self-worth, including our perceptions of our own abilities and looks, as well as our level of contentment in our interpersonal connections. Some individuals have relatively high self-esteem, while others have lower self-esteem, which is partly a quality that is consistent through time. Nevertheless, the level of one's own self-worth may fluctuate from day to day, if not hour to hour. Having high self-esteem comes from having a good self-concept, which includes a lot of positive ideas about ourselves and our accomplishments, as well as feeling accepted and respected by others. Low self-esteem occurs when we have done something detrimental to ourselves, have been neglected, or have felt that we have been chastised.

Why does one have Low Self-Esteem?

Most individuals have a favorable sense of their own self-worth, which may be assessed in two ways: explicitly and implicitly.

In many samples from the Western world, notably in North America, the average score is generally substantially higher than the mid-point. This is an intriguing discovery. Meta-analytic data reveals that fewer than 7% of participants scored below the midpoint. It's possible that people in samples where low self-esteem is measured by a median split really have at least average self-esteem, which has some fascinating implications.

As many individuals, especially in highly individualistic societies, claim to have high self-esteem, the topic of why this is worth exploring. People may feel greater pressure to report feeling good about themselves in certain cultures than in others since some cultures put a higher value on building strong self-esteem. Measures like the Rosenberg scale might be impacted by a desire to show oneself in a favorable light, which is a concern. It's possible that the results of the Rosenberg scale may be exaggerated due to people's tendency to exaggerate their self-esteem in order to seem better than they actually are to the experimenters and to boost their own self-esteem. Self-worth is less of a priority in societies when this is the case; thus, we could expect to see lower self-esteem levels. In fact, this is what most research has shown. The self-esteem levels of Japanese residents in Japan were found by Heine and Lehman to be moderate on average and regularly distributed around the scale's midpoint. According to a slew of research, those from more Western, individualistic cultures have higher self-esteem than those from Eastern, collectivistic cultures. Does this suggest that cultural priorities and pressures play a role in these disparities, or may it be a reflection of true inequalities in self-esteem levels? Of course, there are no simple solutions to this problem, but research employing various techniques of assessing one's own self-esteem has produced some interesting results.

It turns out that the differences in self-esteem among different age groups are rather remarkable.It was discovered via a large-scale Internet survey that the level of self-esteem climbs continuously from early youth through maturity and then starts to fall after that, generally around the age of sixty. We frequently have a better sense of self-worth later in life than we had at the beginning of adulthood, which seems to contradict the ageist stereotype that older people are less self-confident. These age-related improvements in self-esteem may be explained by what? The self-discrepancy hypothesis, which we discussed in the preceding section on the cognitive self, is one alternative. Remember that this theory suggests that we feel better about ourselves when we see the distance between our present and ideal selves as being narrow. Maybe because older folks tend to see themselves in a more idealistic light, they have a stronger sense of self-worth than younger people. Researchers believe this to be the case. This research found that, in comparison to middle-aged and young persons, the elderly had a higher level of similarity between their present and ideal selves. In part, older persons are better equipped than younger ones to realistically adapt their ideal standards as they age and to participate in more positive and age-appropriate social comparisons. This helps older adults to better align their two identities.

Self-Esteem Maintenance and Enhancement

At least in certain cultures, people seem to be encouraged to exaggerate their self-esteem in order to look more confident. Furthermore, as we'll see, they often go out of their way to find a sense of value in others. Research on whether this is a universal cultural desire is ongoing, with some believing that it is, while others dispute if the need for good self-regard is similarly valued in all cultures.

One strategy to boost one's self-esteem is to achieve success in one's career. People who do well on tests, in sports, or in love tend to have more self-esteem than those who don't. Since most of us are typically successful in establishing good lives, this is a factor in our self-esteem. In the event that we fail in one area, we often go on to discover a new one in which we can excel. In school, we don't necessarily expect to be the top student or the best athlete. As a result, when we expect certain things to happen, we are frequently disappointed or harmed. In other words, we're proud of ourselves because we're excellent at making wonderful lives for ourselves and our loved ones.

Building relationships with others is another approach to increase one's self-esteem. In order to feel good about ourselves, we need to be able to form and sustain rewarding relationships. Using social networking sites is a popular method for many individuals across the globe. More and more researches are looking at how this is done online and its influence on our self-worth. We often post status updates on Facebook in the hopes that our friends will "like" or remark on them. However, it might have a detrimental effect on our self-esteem if our friends do not reply to our status posts. Facebook users who were allocated to an experimental scenario where they were prohibited from sharing information on Facebook for 48 hours reported considerably lower feelings of belonging and meaningful existence, according to recent research. Some other half of respondents had their Facebook accounts set up such that they would not get any feedback on their status changes, including "likes" or comments, in the second trial. They reported lower levels of self-esteem, belonging, control, and meaningful life than the control group that did not get feedback. This was in accordance with assumptions. Feeling neglected by our friends, whether online or in-person, may have a negative impact on our self-esteem.

Part of the problem arises from the belief that our self-esteem is very fragile, to begin with, fluctuating on a daily basis, if not hourly. To make things even more complicated, our self-esteem is comprised of both our overall sentiments about ourselves and our feelings about ourselves in particular areas of our life (e.g., as a father, a nurse, a sportsperson, etc.) Generally speaking, the more significant a given area of self-esteem is to us, the larger the influence it has on our overall self-esteem. The fact that someone sighs after tasting the not-so-delicious supper you made will affect a chef's self-esteem considerably more than it would hurt the self-esteem of someone for whom cooking is not a vital part of their identity.

Finally, having a strong sense of self-worth is a positive trait, but only when it is maintained in moderation. Extremely high self-esteem, such as that possessed by narcissists, is often fragile. People in this category may have a positive self-image most of the time, but they are also particularly susceptible to criticism and negative feedback, and their responses to it are often detrimental to their psychological self-development.

Having said that, it is surely feasible to raise our self-esteem if we approach the task in the proper manner. Given below are some strategies for boosting your self-esteem:

Use Positive Thoughts Wisely

The use of constructive pledges such as "I am going to be a great success!" is immensely common, but they have a significant flaw: they tend to make individuals who have poor self-esteem feel even worse about themselves. Why? Because when our self-esteem is low, such assertions are just too diametrically opposed to our pre-existing ideas to be considered valid. Ironically, positive affirmations are effective for a certain population of individuals – those who already have a strong sense of self-worth. For affirmations to be effective when your self-esteem is low, they must be modified to be believed in your mind. Please use "I'm going to be a huge success!" instead." with "I'm going to persist until I succeed!" as an example of positive thinking.

Enhance your Skills

Showing real ability and achievement in phases of our life that are important to us might help us build our self-esteem. If you take pleasure in your ability to prepare delicious meals, host more dinner parties. If you're an excellent runner, you should consider entering races and training for them. In a nutshell, identify your primary strengths and seek out chances and occupations that will allow you to capitalize on them.

Accept praises

One of the hardest elements of developing self-esteem is that when we feel awful about ourselves, we are much more reluctant to compliments — even though it is during these times that we most need them — which makes it much more difficult to achieve. As a result, make it a personal aim to endure praises when you get them, even if they make you feel uncomfortable (and they will). Preparing simple set responses and learning to use them automatically whenever you receive good remarks is the most effective method for preventing the reactive emotions involved with rejecting them (for example, "Thank you" or "How kind of you to say"). Within a short period of time, the temptation to reject or resist praises should diminish — which is also a positive indicator that your self-esteem is becoming stronger.

Replace self-criticism with self-compassion

Regrettably, when our self-esteem is down, we are more inclined to erode it even more by being judgmental of ourselves and our actions. Because our objective is to improve our self-esteem, we must replace self-criticism (which is nearly always completely ineffective, even if it seems persuasive) with self-compassion in order to do thisIn the event that your self-critical inner monologue begins, ask yourself what you would say to a close friend in your situation (we tend to be considerably more compassionate to friends than we are to ourselves), and then direct those words at yourselfThis will prevent you from further harming your self-esteem with critical thoughts and will instead assist you in building it.

Reaffirm your value

Several studies have shown that the following activity may help you recover your self-esteem after it has been damaged: Make a list of the characteristics you possess that are relevant in the particular scenario. In the event that you were rejected by a potential romantic partner, compile a list of the qualities that make you a good relationship possibility (such as being loyal or emotionally available) (you have a strong work ethic or are responsible). Once you've decided on one of the elements on your list, write a short essay (one to two paragraphs) explaining why that particular attribute is significant and likely to be recognized by others in the ahead. Do the workout for a whole week or anytime you feel the need for a boost in your self-esteem.

The bottom line is that enhancing one's self-esteem takes time and effort since it entails adopting and sustaining healthy emotional habits. However, doing so, and particularly doing it effectively, will result in a significant emotional and psychological return on your investment.

Self-adulation and the Limits of Self-Enhancement

From what we've observed so far, it appears that many individuals strive to see themselves as having an optimistic outlook. We exaggerate our strengths and downplay our flaws in order to preserve a healthy sense of self-worth. It's conceivable to provide an abnormal amount of self-esteem if that self-esteem is unrealistic and unearned. Overly high levels of self-esteem, adulation, and self-centeredness define narcissism.

At first glance, narcissists may seem endearing, but with time, they tend to alienate those around them. Also, since they are more prone than non-narcissists to be disloyal and act selfishly in love relationships, narcissists may make lousy romantic partners. Narcissists, on the other hand, are more inclined to intimidate people and react angrily to any criticism they get. Individuals with sociopathic tendencies are more inclined to engage in self-serving actions, which may have a negative impact on others and their communities. However, narcissists seem to be aware of these facts about themselves, and they continue to participate in the activities despite this knowledge. Over the last several decades, some nations have observed a rise in the number of people with narcissistic personality characteristics.. The societal consequences of these characteristics make this news alarming. Child-centered parenting styles, the rise in the cult of celebrity, and social media's role in encouraging personal self-enhancement are all factors that contribute to this trend, according to researchers. The availability of easy credit is also cited as a contributing factor in the rise in the sense of entitlement that people feel because they have access to status-related goods. It should come as no surprise that persons from individualistic cultures are more likely than those from collectivistic cultures to exhibit narcissistic features, given that narcissism is rooted in an excessive sense of self-worth.

Because of the negative effects of narcissism, it's fascinating to consider whether or not having a strong sense of self-worth is always beneficial to ourselves and others around us. The Rosenberg Scale, for example, does not discriminate between persons who have a reasonable and healthy sense of self-esteem and those who have inflated, even narcissistic, views of themselves. Also, implicit assessments don't provide a clear picture, although there is evidence to suggest that more narcissistic persons score higher on implicit self-esteem in relation to certain attributes, such as social standing, and lower on other traits related to interpersonal connections. Realistic vs. unrealistically high self-esteem has different impacts, and this may be difficult to discern. Nonetheless, we'll now devote our attention to this knotty problem.

High Self-Esteem: A Cause of Happiness

The belief that strong self-esteem has a good impact on people's lives is widely held by educators, parents, school counselors, and individuals in a wide range of cultures. Increasing your self-esteem may help you perform better at work or attract a more attractive companion, according to the theory that self-esteem can be improved. A lot of people share your sentiments. The self-esteem movement, as it is known by researchers, has increased in prominence in numerous nations since the 1970s, and they outline its roots and current pace. According to a task commission financed by the State of California in 1986, improving self-esteem would help alleviate many of the state's issues, including crime, adolescent pregnancy, drug addiction, and school underachievement, as well as polluting the air.

Study after a study looked at the evidence to see whether or not having high self-esteem is as beneficial as many people believe. After determining which characteristics were associated with high self-esteem, they looked at how much of a role high self-esteem had in causing the results they were interested in. Having a strong sense of self-worth, the researchers found, is linked to a wide range of positive outcomes. Having a strong sense of self-worth has been linked to increased initiative and activity; people with a high sense of self-worth just do more.They are also more likely than persons with poor self-esteem to protect victims from bullies, and they are also more inclined to begin connections and speak out in groups than the latter. Those with a high level of self-esteem are also more likely to try new things if they fail at the first one they try.Happier, more active, and more equipped to deal with their circumstances are those who have greater levels of self-esteem.

Researchers observed that those with exceptionally high self-esteem reacted more harshly, hostile, and arrogantly when they were forced to fail on a challenging assignment in front of a partner. As a result, narcissistic children are more likely to engage in aggressive behavior than non-narcissistic youngsters. In light of these results, it's possible that programs aimed at boosting the self-esteem of youngsters who bully and are violent may actually do more damage than good. These outcomes may not be a surprise to social psychologists, who know that narcissists prioritize their own interests above those of others and that caring about others is essential for healthy interpersonal relationships. When Baumeister and his colleagues examined the causative function of self-esteem, they found no evidence that high self-esteem produced these beneficial outcomes, in spite of the numerous positive characteristics that are associated with it. For example, although academic success and strong self-esteem are linked, the latter is more the outcome than the cause of the former. Academic performance has not been improved by programs aimed at improving the self-esteem of students, and laboratory experiments have typically failed to demonstrate that manipulating self-esteem causes better task performance.

Researchers came to the conclusion that self-esteem programs should be utilized sparingly and shouldn't be the only strategy used. Raising one's self-esteem will not improve one's grades in school, follow the law, avoid difficulty, or respect the rights of others. When self-esteem is boosted, it may even lead to narcissism or conceit. Researchers believe that boosting children's self-esteem should only be used as a reward for good conduct and meaningful accomplishments rather than as a way to make them feel better about themselves.

Reclaiming Self-Respect

When it comes to matters of one's self-respect, most individuals tend to operate from an emotional rather than a rational perspective. People often do and say things they would never do or say if they weren't experiencing the pain of grief and loss. The worst thing about ending a relationship with somebody you care about is realizing how much you hate yourself in the process. You can't begin the process of healing after a horrible breakup unless you are ready to accept who you are.

Here are three suggestions for regaining your sense of dignity and self-worth:

Set clear limits for yourself

In the aftermath of a breakup, it may be difficult to reestablish your emotional equilibrium since setting boundaries might seem like you're giving in to the pain of separation. Having clearly defined boundaries does not need a complete break from the other person, although it may be the best way to do this. As a result of establishing clear boundaries, you behave in a manner that is respectful to yourself and congruent with the current relationship you have, rather than the previous one. You didn't continue to give of yourself in the same way as you do now while you were together. Unless you've previously lived together, you no longer allow the other to act as if you still do, and you're not in a physical relationship with someone who is not fully committed to you and doesn't have your best interests at heart, you can expect the other person to handle their own errands and household duties without your assistance. These are all indications that the other individual isn't the appropriate one for your situation. The other person's feelings will not be hurt by this, but you will be able to take the time and space you need for yourself.

Forgive

Nothing is worse than dwelling on the bad things that have happened to you or the things that you have done in the past that you may now wish you hadn't done. To liberate oneself from the past, you must accept it as it is and go on. The ability to forgive is a crucial part of learning to let go. Self-empowerment is at the heart of forgiveness, not letting someone else off the hook for their terrible actions. When you forgive someone, you remove the power they have over you to be wounded again in the future. Recognizing that what other people do is a direct reflection of who they are and has nothing to do with you may be a good thing to remember. As a result of someone's betrayal or dishonesty, it does not mean that you are incompetent. A guy who criticizes you for their behavior demonstrates a lack of self-awareness, not the other way around. Because most individuals do not want to harm others, they act out of a sense of self-preservation. When you realize that someone else's actions aren't always personal, it may help ease the pain and make it easier to put the past behind you.

Focus on yourself

You'll probably have more free time after a breakup. Consider working on yourself instead of immediately looking for a new companion to fill the vacuum. You don't want to meet your future spouse when you're a complete emotional wreck.Spend more time at the gym, purchase new clothing, or get a new haircut to look and feel better about yourself. Try something new, whether it's taking a class or attending a presentation on personal development or something you've always wanted to learn about. Your focus will shift away from your ex-girlfriend and onto something else entirely while you're out and about doing things that make you feel good about yourself.

Though the pain of ending a relationship may be excruciating if you redirect your attention to valuing oneself and feeling positive about who and what you are, it's impossible not to create new opportunities and meet new people who share your values.

Examples of People with Strong Self-Esteem

Everyone on this list may have succumbed to a poor sense of self-worth. As an alternative, they choose to overcome significant obstacles as well as traumatic experiences and thoughts. Those who have overcome their difficulties may do the same for you, too.

Helen Keller (1880–1968)

Until she was around 1-and-a-half years old, she had excellent vision and hearing.Due to her symptoms, scarlet fever or meningitis are the most likely diagnoses. After that, she lost her ability to see and hear fully.

When she was six years old, her first teacher, Anne Sullivan, came. She was enrolled as a student on her first day at the school. She and her instructor then traveled to New York so that she could attend a school for the deaf there. She began attending Radcliffe College at the age of 20 after attending The Cambridge School for Young Ladies at the age of 14. Just at the age of twenty-four, she became the first deaf and blind person to get a bachelor's degree from Radcliffe College.

She became a world-famous public speaker, advocating for global peace, civil rights, labor rights, women's rights, and birth control, among other causes. She was also a prolific writer on these subjects, having penned several books and articlesPresidency Lyndon B. Johnson honoured her in 1964 by presenting her with the Presidential Medal of Freedom. In the year following her election, she was also inducted into the National Women's

Hall of Fame in New York City.The Alabama Women's Hall of Fame inducted her in 1971.

Thomas Edison (1847–1931)

Only three months of Edison's life were spent in school. A lack of understanding of how Edison's mind operated caused his instructor to conclude that he was mentally impaired. And Edison's health deteriorated rapidly from childhood on.

Edison was tutored by his mother, who worked as a teacher. Edison's life was forever changed by an event that occurred while he was only a teenager. He was deaf after being sucked onto a speeding train by his ears.

His first innovation, an electronic voting system, was patented when he was 21 years old. At the end of one four-year period, he averaged one new patent every five days, which was his aim. He was regarded as "the Wonder of Menlo Park" because of how productive his lab was.

For example, phonograph, motion picture, and light bulb were all developed at Edison's laboratory. The General Electric Company was the name given to his electric company throughout time. Isn't this a brilliant idea?

Harriet Tubman (around 1822–1913)

As the fifth of nine children, Harriet Tubman was raised as a slave.She and her brothers fled slavery when she was 27 years old. Her brothers came back and compelled her to return. Using the Underground Railroad, an informal, well-organized system of free blacks, slaves, and white abolitionist abolitionists, Mary fled to Philadelphia a second time, this time without her siblings.

The Union Army used Tubman as a cook and nurse, then as a scout and spy during the Civil War. More than 750 slaves in South Carolina were freed on her first armed expedition of the Civil War, which included three steamboats.

Tubman went to New York, Boston, and Washington, D.C., in her latter years to advocate for women's right to vote. She was a member of suffragist groups and worked with Susan B. Anthony at meetings. After Tubman spoke at the NFAW inaugural meeting, the organization was renamed after her.

Chapter 8

Mediation And Affirmations To "Put Yourself First"

Positive Affirmations and Meditation Can Be Beneficial During a Coronavirus Infection.

What are positive affirmations and how do they work?Positive affirmations are sentences that you repeat to yourself that depict a certain result or define who you want to be in a particular situation. It is your brain's utilization of these words, ideas, or attitudes that allow it to overcome negative thoughts and reprogram your mentality. The term is originated from the Latin verb affirmare, which literally translates as "to grow strong or durable."

People have relied on the power of self-affirmation to propel them forward in their lives since the dawn of time. As far back as thousands of years ago, affirmations might be found in spiritual literature and holy books.

It is critical to note that positive affirmations or any form of self-talk should not be centred on the negative, denial, or refusal to accept that anything occurred. Recently, the coronavirus has been reported as a negative occurrence; nevertheless, you embrace the truth of what is occurring and use affirmations to help you respond and react to your sentiments in a more positive manner. Consider the following statements: "I have faith in my capacity to get through difficult circumstances," or "I will not obsess about things I have no control over."

When you are able to concentrate on the positive aspects of your personality, your inherent strength may emerge, allowing you to better deal with and find answers to life's issues in a healthy way. Those are abilities and powers we were born with; all we have to do is trust what science has to say about them. It all starts with the good things we say to ourselves in order to make our lives happier, to better connect with our loved ones, and to have a greater feeling of appreciation and satisfaction.

It is possible to locate several positive affirmation phrases, as well as compose a particular statement based on your present needs on a post-it note. Make sure you have access to your written affirmation on a regular basis and that you think about it multiple times every day.

Make things as simple as possible. It is not suitable to recite the phrases such as "cannot" and "will not." Always have a cheerful attitude and remain in the current moment. Don't hold your past or the future of things. The brain only reacts to the current moment – it responds really effectively to what is occurring right now and in the present moment.

Using words such as "heal" or sentiments like "I'm peaceful," "I'm confident," or "We will get through this together" in your affirmations will help you feel better. The habit of affirmation has been scientifically shown to signal the brain and body to perform at their highest levels when confronted with a problem.

Brain Activity After negative thoughts

In all, human bodies contain more than 37.2 trillion cells, or one hundred times as many stars as there are in our galaxy, is a huge quantity. To put it another way, they act as a conduit for communication between the nervous system and the brain. It should be no surprise that the mind is continually cycling through your ideas, both consciously and subconsciously, as a result of all of this activity. There have been scientific studies conducted that reveal that the typical individual experiences at least 45 negative stress responses every day.

The mental conversation we have with ourselves is often depressing and discouraging. It's normal to not even be aware that you're saying negative things to yourself, such as "I'm no good," "I can't survive this," "The coronavirus is going to wreck my life," or "I'm not up to it." It's important to recognize when you're saying negative things to yourself. The trouble is that we don't do nearly enough to counteract those bad feelings. Our negative internal monologues cause a range of emotions such as wrath, fear, and humiliation to be triggered.

Every idea you have right now has an impact on your brain cells because neurons in the connections that are developing between them are being affected. If your ideas are causing you to feel nervous, various emotions will be triggered, including anxiety, tension, fear, and concern. "These 'fight-or-flight' responses from your hypothalamic-pituitary-adrenal complex cause an excessive release of stress hormones into your body," says the author.

Even if there isn't an emergency, your body's emergency response mechanism is activated throughout this procedure. For the brain, your ideas and visions become a physical reality. As a basic example, you may feel terror when watching a terrifying movie. While watching a movie, genuine physiological responses in your body might be caused by stress hormones, which cause your heart rate to rise even if you are aware that the movie is not real.

Chronic stress responses may even cause changes in your body's chemistry. For example, stress might have an impact on the ageing process. Your chromosomes disintegrate at a quicker rate, which is why those who suffer from severe, chronic stress have a shorter life expectancy. Finding healthy strategies to manage unfavourable interactions between your brain and body may have a good influence on your overall health and well-being.

Mind-body balance may be achieved by the backdoor method of balancing brain and body. This manifests itself in your thoughts, attitude, goals, words, actions, and behaviours, as well as how you react to the challenges of life. Your affirmations are created in response to the needs that you are experiencing at the time.

Self Affirmations

Self-confidence and self-worth are boosted by affirmations, and here are 19 of the best!

Simply choose one of the following confidence-boosting affirmations:

- I am self-assured and believe in my abilities.

- New chances for growth and development are available every day.
- I have the power to influence the course of history.
- I have the ability to accomplish everything I set my mind to.
- I am self-assured in my ability.
- With each new difficulty, I learn something new.
- My dedication to my job is unwavering.
- I already have or can quickly get all I need to be successful.
- I choose to let go of limiting ideas and put my faith in myself.
- My capabilities are limitless.
- I am certain that I can handle any task with ease and that there is nothing I cannot conquer.
- Every every day, I work towards living the life of my dreams.
- Every day, I come to work and give it my all.
- I have confidence in my talents and am able to express myself freely.
- Everything I need to be successful is already inside me.

- I have complete power over my life.
- Positive self-talk and the desire for others' approval have been replaced by self-acceptance.
- I am sufficient for myself.
- I've decided to put my faith in the process.

A Message for All the Readers

Please accept my sincere thanks for taking the time to learn about self-esteem.

It is imperative that you take away just one crucial lesson from this piece: you can undoubtedly improve your own self-esteem, and you can significantly influence the self-esteem of individuals you care about.

Building self-esteem won't make your life easy or devoid of hardships and disappointments, but it will give you the confidence to attempt new things, the resiliency to bounce back from setbacks, and the openness to achievement that will help you achieve your goals..

It's something we'll have to keep working towards, but it's something that's certainly attainable.

Continue to be dedicated and committed.

Maintain awareness of your mental thoughts as well as your exterior environment.

Maintain your focus on your own objectives and all that is achievable when self-doubt is not a hindrance.

What are your ideas on the topic of self-esteem in psychological studies?

It means a lot that you took the time to read this!